GW01606150

SELECTED POEMS OF THOMAS HARDY

THE POETRY BOOKSHELF

General Editor: James Reeves

Robert Graves: *English and Scottish Ballads*
James Reeves: *Chaucer: Lyric and Allegory*
Tom Scott: *Late Medieval Scots Poetry*
William Tydeman: *English Poetry 1400–1580*
Martin Seymour-Smith: *Shakespeare's Sonnets*
Martin Seymour-Smith: *Longer Elizabethan Poems*
James Reeves: *John Donne*
Maurice Hussey: *Jonson and the Cavaliers*
Jack Dalglish: *Eight Metaphysical Poets*
James Reeves and Martin Seymour-Smith: *Andrew Marvell*
Denis Burden: *Shorter Poems of John Milton*
V. de S. Pinto: *Poetry of the Restoration*
Roger Sharrock: *John Dryden*
James Reeves: *Jonathan Swift*
John Heath-Stubbs: *Alexander Pope*
Francis Venables: *The Early Augustans*
Donald Davie: *The Late Augustans*
Donald Davie: *Augustan Lyrics*
James Reeves: *Thomas Gray*
F. W. Bateson: *William Blake*
G. S. Fraser: *Robert Burns*
Roger Sharrock: *Willaim Wordsworth*
James Reeves: *S. T. Coleridge*
Robin Skelton: *Lord Byron*
John Holloway: *P. B. Shelley*
James Reeves: *John Clare*
Robert Gittings: *Poems and Letters of John Keats*
James Reeves: *Five Late Romantic Poets*
Edmund Blunden: *Alfred Lord Tennyson*
James Reeves: *Robert Browning*
Denys Thompson: *Poems and Prose of Matthew Arnold*
James Reeves: *Emily Dickinson*
James Reeves: *G. M. Hopkins*
David Wright: *Seven Victorian Poets*
James Reeves and Martin Seymour-Smith: *Walt Whitman*
James Reeves: *The Modern Poets' World*
James Reeves and Robert Gittings: *Thomas Hardy*
James Reeves: *D. H. Lawrence*

SELECTED POEMS OF THOMAS HARDY

Edited with an Introduction and Notes

by

JAMES REEVES

and

ROBERT GITTINGS

HEINEMANN: LONDON
BARNES & NOBLE: TOTOWA, NEW JERSEY

Heinemann Educational Books Ltd
22 Bedford Square, London WC1B 3HH
LONDON EDINBURGH MELBOURNE AUCKLAND
HONG KONG SINGAPORE KUALA LUMPUR NEW DELHI
IBADAN NAIROBI JOHANNESBURG KINGSTON
PORT OF SPAIN

THOMAS HARDY 1840–1928

First published 1981

Published in the USA by Barnes & Noble Books 1981

British Library C. I. P. Data

Hardy, Thomas, *b. 1840*
Selected poems of Thomas Hardy.—
(Poetry bookshelf).
I. Reeves, James II. Gittings, Robert
III. Series
821'.8 PR4740

ISBN 0–435–15076–6
ISBN (USA) 0–389–20080–8

Printed and bound in Great Britain by
Morrison & Gibb Ltd, London and Edinburgh

CONTENTS

PUBLISHER'S NOTE ix
CRITICAL INTRODUCTION x
BIOGRAPHICAL INTRODUCTION xxiii
SELECTED POEMS:
After a Journey 1
Afternoon Service at Mellstock 2
Afterwards 2
An August Midnight 3
At Castle Boterel 4
At the Word 'Farewell' 5
Autumn in King's Hintock Park 6
Beeny Cliff 7
Beyond the Last Lamp 9
Birds at Winter Nightfall 10
A Bird-Scene at a Rural Dwelling 11
A Broken Appointment 11
The Choirmaster's Burial 12
Christmas: 1924 14
A Commonplace Day 14
A Confession to a friend in Trouble 15
The Conformers 16
The Convergence of the Twain 17
Copying Architecture in an Old Minster 19
The Darkling Thrush 20
The Dead Man Walking 22
A Death-Day Recalled 23
The Dream Is—Which? 24
Drummer Hodge 25
During Wind and Rain 25
The Eve of Waterloo 26
The Five Students 28
Friends Beyond 29
The Going 31

Great Things 32
Green Slates 33
The Haunter 34
Her Dilemma 35
Heredity 36
Horses Aboard 36
The House of Hospitalities 37
I Am the One 37
I Found Her Out There 38
I Have Lived with Shades 40
I Look into my Glass 41
The Impercipient 42
In a Waiting Room 43
In Church 44
In the British Museum 45
In the Cemetery 46
In Time of 'The Breaking Of Nations' 47
Lament 47
The Later Autumn 49
The Levelled Churchyard 49
Life and Death at Sunrise 50
Logs on the Hearth 51
Men Who March Away 52
Midnight on the Great Western 53
The Missed Train 54
Molly Gone 55
Nature's Questioning 56
Near Lanivet, 1872 57
Neutral Tones 58
The Night of Trafalgar 59
A Night in November 60
Nobody Comes 60
No Buyers 61
Not Only I 62
Old Furniture 63
On a Midsummer Eve 64
The Oxen 64
Paths of Former Time 65
Paying Calls 66

The Phantom Horsewoman 67
The Prospect 68
Proud Songsters 69
Rain on a Grave 69
Regret Not Me 70
Reminiscences of a Dancing Man 72
The Ruined Maid 73
The Second Visit 74
Self-Unconscious 74
The Self-Unseeing 76
A Sheep Fair 76
The Shiver 77
Snow in the Suburbs 78
Something Tapped 79
A Spot 79
The Sunshade 80
Thoughts of Phena 81
A Trampwoman's Tragedy 82
Transformations 86
Under the Waterfall 86
The Voice 88
Voices from Things Growing in a Churchyard 89
We are Getting to the End 90
Weathers 91
We Field-Women 92
We Sat at the Window 92
Wessex Heights 93
When I Set Out for Lyonnesse 95
When Oats Were Reaped 95
Where the Picnic Was 96
The Whitewashed Wall 97
Who's in the Next Room 98
The Wind's Prophecy 99
The Year's Awakening 100
The Young Glass-stainer 101
Zermatt: to the Matterhorn 101
NOTES 103
INDEX OF FIRST LINES 111

PUBLISHER'S NOTE

The selection of poems and Critical Introduction for this book were completed by James Reeves just before his death in 1978. He had for many years wanted to include a Hardy selection in the Poetry Bookshelf series, of which he was General Editor for over a quarter of a century. It was fitting that the last piece of work he did should have been on a poet so dear to his heart.

It was always intended that this book should be jointly edited by Robert Gittings, author of *Young Thomas Hardy, The Older Hardy* and (with Jo Manton) *The Second Mrs. Hardy*. Dr. Gittings has supplied the Biographical Introduction and seen the book through the press.

The poems are arranged alphabetically by title throughout.

CRITICAL INTRODUCTION

by James Reeves

The definitive edition of Hardy's poems contains nine hundred and forty-seven items, excluding the long verse drama, *The Dynasts.* With this I am not now concerned. Nor am I concerned with the novels and tales, which are in themselves a gigantic achievement, enough to earn any writer a permanent reputation, as they did. But of course the mind of the novelist is also the mind of the poet. I wouldn't quarrel with anyone who defined the novels as poems under another guise. Hardy's evocative power of natural description and his exploration of private feeling are more akin to what we associate with lyric poetry than to what we associate with narrative, which may be why Proust admired him as he did. Hardy's poems and novels interpenetrate at many points. His decision, after the critics' hostile reception of his last novel, *Jude the Obscure,* in 1895, to abandon prose fiction and devote all his powers to poetry, was crucial, both for himself and for English poetry. He was, in effect, a Victorian novelist but a twentieth-century poet, in my opinion the greatest. About half of his poetic output was written after his sixtieth birthday in 1900, but the other half, composed or drafted intermittently during the previous forty years, was extensively revised in the twentieth century.

The sheer bulk of his output makes it difficult to take a coherent view of his poems as a whole. Selection is essential: what this book contains is a personal choice. Indeed every reader's choice of Hardy's poems must be personal. I have read much critical commentary, and there is very little agreement as to which are the best. The various selections published over the years exhibit what, to many readers, are glaring omissions and equally incomprehensible inclusions. Everyone is agreed that Hardy was a great poet, but there is no agreement as to what constitutes his greatness. It might be well, before getting entangled in a semantic web, to quote F. R. Leavis's judgement that 'His rank as a major poet rests upon a dozen poems'. This is, to say the least, cautious—even evasive. I don't know if Leavis changed his view in the subsequent fifty years (although he went so far as to include a sharply penetrating account of *After a Journey* in his book *The Living Principle* (1975)); it should be noted in passing that the word 'major' has no more objectivity than has 'great'. It is rather like saying that the Alps owe their rank as a major climbing area to a few peaks — Mont Blanc, the Matterhorn, the Jungfrau. Analogies and metaphors can be misleading and must not be pushed too far, but the summits of Hardy's achievement could not exist without the lesser peaks, the upper and lower slopes, the foothills, and even the valleys where feebleness and bathos are found. Hardy's poems, to anyone who has considered them as a whole, must be seen as not unlike the Alps, a whole country or region whose size and variety are breathtaking.

The sheer variety of reaction among intelligent readers is, I think, evidence of the vitality—the *livingness*—of the poems. To discuss them with any such reader is to discover what has become, to me, an absolute certainty—that every reader has his own conception of Hardy the poet. This is because the poems exert their own magical spell differently on every individual. Every reader's personal Hardy is in some measure a reflection or projection of himself. Of no other English poet can this be said, except of Shakespeare.

My own view of Hardy's poems, based on the experience of at least fifty years' familiarity, reinforced and deepened by reading the whole corpus in recent months, will emerge in what follows. Poetry has been defined, by whom I don't know, as 'memorable speech'. We must discover what Hardy's speech is about, what aspects of it are most characteristic, what constitutes the essential elements for the poet—where, so to speak, his priorities are. We must also consider the qualities of 'memorability' in our preferred poems. There are some readers who look for what is called Hardy's philosophy. They look for Hardy the thinker. Some always look for thought or *Weltanschauung* or philosophy in poetry. I propose to look for, and to exhibit, Hardy the poet at his best and most characteristic.

In looking for the essential poetry of any poet, it is necessary to discover his individual sensibility as a man. The core of Hardy's concern with humanity and its problems, its burdens, its successes and failures, is a continuous introspective concern—you could almost say 'obsession'—with what Wordsworth called 'his own passions and volitions'. Consider *Great Things* (p. 32). A poem with such a title, you might expect, would tell us something, if not much, about its author. It is not perhaps a great poem, but only the Hardy of greater poems could have written it: it is an affirmation of the conviction that the simple pleasures of youth are at the heart of a healthy feeling for life.

But life on this uncomplicated level is not the whole story. Any poet—indeed any person,—must be simultaneously aware of its completion, its fruition and its negation: death. Hardy, like Emily Dickinson, was continuously occupied with the fact of death. Only if we look death in the face, almost in an attitude of defiance, can life be fully lived and apprehended. The poem *Afterwards* (p. 2) has always been to me one of the peaks of Hardy's poetry and, because of its form, one of the most memorable poems. In its five stanzas Hardy imagines how friends and neighbours will receive the news of his death, whether it comes in early summer; in the dusk; in a warm late summer night; or in the darkness of a frosty winter night. The poem as a whole is at once self-regarding—it is his own death that he is thinking of—and outward-looking. How well, he is wondering, does his community really know him? His mind ranges over the course of the year, and his own special preoccupations. First, he is an observer of the details of nature—

like the sheen on new leaves; next he sees himself as one who used to exercise a brooding, continuous observation of the life of the animals—the hawk and the hedgehog—for whom he exerted an active and compassionate care. Then he records his lifelong interest in the cosmos—the 'full-starred heavens'. At the end he wonders if he is thought of as a man with a keen ear, alert to the refinements of sound—the pauses made by a crossing breeze in the otherwise continuous tolling of his passing bell in the night. In this way there is a masterly integration of the thought of his actual moment of death with the contemplation, first, of his own image as a social being, and then of the facts of his own concern with vegetable and animal life in its humbler aspect and the whole cosmos from earth to outer space.

Before considering other poems which illustrate these various interests, something should be said about Hardy's style and the qualities of 'memorability' which make this poem quintessential. First, the loose, unemphatic rhythm—something between speech and rhetoric; secondly, the almost flat naturalness, the unaffected underemphasis of such lines as 'He was a man who used to notice such things', which is a touchstone of the essential Hardy; next, the precision of the diction, and the matter-of-factness of statement; and lastly, a sort of wistful resignation in the tone.

He strove that innocent creatures should come to no harm,
But he could do little for them: and now he is gone.

C. Day Lewis, a poet with a profound admiration for Hardy, puts his finger on an important point about his style when he says: 'One can think of few less promising lines to start a poem—or more ponderous ways of saying "When I am dead"—than "When the present has latched its postern behind my tremulous stay"; yet the poem it begins is one of Hardy's finest' (see *The Lyrical Poetry of Thomas Hardy,* 1951).

Reading it again, one can see that this 'ponderous' opening has a sort of incantatory magic which ensures attention for the quiet, colloquial undertone of what is to follow. Many writers have commented, often adversely, on the freakishness, the quirks and oddities of Hardy's style. This freakishness is something which at first we find surprising and then learn to love, even when it amuses us, as we learn to accept and enjoy the idiosyncrasies of a friend. We have to learn to accept Hardy as he was, 'warts and all'. Some critics have been patronising about his oddities of style, excusing them on the ground that he was an autodidact without formal education. It is true that he seems sometimes to lack a sense of self-criticism, but on the whole he had a shrewd awareness of what he was doing. Professor Donald Davie, writing of Hardy's verse technique, says that he was 'an honest journeyman'. A 'journeyman' is defined as an artisan between the ranks of apprentice and master, licensed to work as a day-labourer. With this in mind consider the short, intensively personal poem called *A Broken Appointment* (p. 11).

The two stanzas of this poem are perfectly matched in formal symmetry; the language is restrained and precise, the feeling powerful but controlled. The word-order is absolutely natural and inevitable, despite the demands of a fairly tight rhyme-scheme. It is as near perfection as can be desired. Is this the work of a journeyman beneath the rank of 'master'? I would like to amend Professor Davie's egregious phrase and say that Hardy was unquestionably a master and, being a true poet, was not always honest. He was no artisan but a craftsman of hand-made products. He succeeds all the better by exploiting the waywardness of his medium, the English language—the irregularities, the surprises, the knots and grains of the wood—what Blake called 'the rough basement'. *A Broken Appointment* is a triumph, first because of its formal perfection, the perfection of an artefact that can be handled in the mind, giving pleasure to the mind's sense of touch; and also because it is an expression of profound feeling, transcending the egoistic grievance of a man who has been let down by a woman, and raising his sense of wrong to communicate sympathetically with anyone who has suffered in the same way. A good and very dignified poem is thus composed, not for the writer but for humanity. No doubt the woman who 'did not come' had her point of view, but that is not the matter in hand.

Indeed, the sexes might almost have been interchanged. Hardy slips into the feelings of the opposite sex with natural ease. We often have to read far on into a poem in autobiographical form to discover that it is written in the person of a woman. Another poem, *Her Dilemma* (p. 35) slight though it is, gives the feeling of a woman prepared to tell a lie 'for pure loving-kindness' sake'.

Returning to the study of the key poem *Afterwards,* it can be seen how each succeeding stanza illustrates an aspect of Hardy's nature which inspired him again and again throughout his long poetic life. Perhaps the most pervasive feature of his consciousness as a poet is his sense of an instinctive communion with all life, human, animal, vegetable—and even mineral. He is no mere bystander, even though he appears passive. His apparent passivity is always compassionate. He makes the claim very explicitly in the poem *I am the one* (p. 37).

An August Midnight (p. 3) expresses Hardy's feelings for the humblest creatures, creatures of the insect world. This feeling is of mingled gratitude, respect and community. Notice the words 'Thus meet we five . . . at this point of time in this point of space'. This reaches out to another recurrent theme in Hardy's thinking which readers of the novels will readily recognise—the theme of coincidence in time and place.

Hardy's unequalled objectivity combined with his esemplastic power, his simultaneous contemplation of men and their natural surroundings, are brilliantly displayed in *The Later Autumn* (p. 49). He is at his best when his eye is firmly, almost piercingly, on the object. This objectivity, Wordsworthian in its purity, amounts to a virtually selfless identification with Nature. But this is never divided from his sense of form. In *A Bird-Scene at a Rural Dwelling* (p. 11) his shaping mind, in a way that recalls some Chinese poetry, first gives us the visual essentials of a rural scene which seems general or universal, and then proceeds to extract from it a sense of continuity made, one might say, palpable in one particular dwelling.

This feeling for the passage of time is another important element in Hardy's total consciousness. The 'bird scene' so graphically and sparingly presented links humble creation with humble people in a time span of a hundred years. In another short poem of the same quality—*Birds at Winter Nightfall* (p. 10)—the poet, as it were, identifies himself with birds. This is another similarity between Hardy and Emily Dickinson. Notice how, almost triumphantly, he here gets away with the coinage 'crumb-outcaster', the birds eye view of a familiar cottage-dweller.

Hardy uses his empathy with birds once more in a famous and even controversial poem, *The Darkling Thrush* (p. 20), written in 1900, to express his feelings on the turn of the century and on his sixtieth year. This epitaph on the nineteenth century has been praised and condemned in equal measure. A very favourable view of the poem is taken by John Bayley in his *An Essay on Hardy* (Cambridge 1978). Professor Davie, on the other hand, writes it off as an 'anthology piece', a term often used by the sophisticated as an automatic condemnation. If there have to be anthologies, they have to contain 'pieces'. But a poem is not good or bad because it is frequently anthologised. For me, *The Darkling Trush* is perfectly, even poignantly, observed, and the self-identification of the poet and the singer 'frail, gaunt and small' is irresistible and infinitely pathetic. The later Hardy often wrote of himself as frail and small. We recall 'When the present has latched its postern behind my *tremulous* stay'. The irony of the reference in the last line to a 'hope . . . whereof I was unaware' is part of the 'Hardy the pessimist' myth to which I don't propose to pay much attention.

In another 'anthology piece', *Weathers,* we return to the wider sense of community with the cosmos which we found in *Afterwards*. *Weathers* (p. 91) is a technical success which, like some successes in music—for example, the small masterpieces of Mozart—looks bewilderingly easy. Early summer is contrasted with late autumn in a series of pictures in which the poet expresses his sense of communion with vegetable, animal and human participants. The repeated refrain 'And so do I', which might sound mechanical, is a master-stroke. It may be noticed in passing that every image in this poem except one ('the unseen throbbing of the hidden tides') is visual. If this poem is in every school anthology, so much the better for the children.

Another of Hardy's interests, as recorded in *Afterwards,* was the celestial bodies, from the moon to outer space. He wanted to be remembered as a man fascinated by 'the full-starred heavens' in winter. It is the measure of his comprehensive cosmic view, from the fly that settles on his writing to the farthest stars. The supposed influence of the stars on human affairs was one of the persistent folk-beliefs which partly provided the substitute religion of a rationalist. The stars are a factor in a strange poem entitled *The Shiver* (p. 77). This poem is one of many in which Hardy the novelist summarises, in the person of a woman, a crucial incident in a human relationship. At another time he might have made it into a short story. Hardy's preoccupation with micro- and macro-cosmic phenomena is clearly evident in a poem inspired by a visit to Zermatt in the Swiss Alps and by the conquest of the Matterhorn in 1865—*Zermatt: to the Matterhorn* (p. 101). It is one of the best of his public poems—poems based less on personal feeling than on an event in history. I care less for these poems than for more intimate ones, but here his ranging and brooding mind is fully occupied by tragedy and heroism, and by the long history of Europe from Biblical to Victorian times.

Even this, among the best of his public poems, is not wholly satisfactory. I turn with relief and confidence to a poem which is intensely personal—*I Look into my Glass* (p. 41). It is at the other end of the Hardy spectrum. This is, to me, essential Hardy. I have known it for fifty years, and can readily say it by heart, especially when I am feeling sorry for myself. Is self-pity, then, a habit to be admired or condemned? I think most professions have some typical trait or fault. Bacon, decrying ambition in general as a sin, said that 'to take a soldier without ambition is to pull off his spurs'. Self-pity in a poet can be a virtue, because he is putting into words his own experience of self-pity for the benefit of everyone. Hardy in old age works off his self-pity in a beautiful and dignified poem. Coleridge, a century earlier, was prone to self-pity and could wallow in it. But often it emerged in the form of poetry which speaks for all of us.

> Alone, alone, all, all alone,
> Alone on a wide, wide sea,
> And never a saint took pity on
> My soul in agony.

Hardy's reference to his 'fragile frame' looks back to those other revealing words, 'frail' and 'tremulous'.

Not only was Hardy's mind one which held space, near and far, in simultaneous contemplation; its range over time, too, was all-embracing. The simultaneity of his earliest memories, his middle and his later years, must strike any reader. His poems scarcely exhibit any chronological development in the ordinary sense. He speculated, as much as any thinking man, on the future, but only as a continuation of the present and the past. He had, as we have seen, a passionate interest in the continuity of things, and, in particular, things and people. Humanity was always his main concern. *Heredity* (p. 36) expresses very directly his conviction about the continuity of all human life. It is not so much a biological as a biographical statement. Hardy was always interested in his own family connections and in his roots in the life and people of his childhood and youth; but his views were physical, not metaphysical. Much of his early training as an architect was spent in churches and churchyards. Among the best of his poems are the churchyard ones, such as *Transformations* (p. 86). Not only were the people of his youth ever-present to his vision and thinking; so also were the things they had used. He dwelt on old things, not as a casual museum visitor, but because they were for ever instinct with the lives of human beings. Better than anyone, Hardy could feelingly dramatise the souls of old musical instruments in a museum.

Here is one stanza of *Haunting Fingers,* subtitled *A Fantasy in a Museum of Musical Instruments:*

> And they felt past handlers clutch them;
> Though none was in the room,
> Old players' dead fingers touch them,
> Shrunk in the tomb.

A similar but more successful poem is *Old Furniture* (p. 63)

A key poem in which Hardy's feelings about the continuity of past and present are expressed most memorably is *Friends Beyond* (p. 29). One reason for the compulsion which this poem has exercised over generations of readers is the incantatory, almost trance-like rhythm of the ghosts' speech:

> In the muted, measured note
> Of a ripple under archways, or a lone cave's stillicide:
> 'We have triumphed: this achievement turns the bane to antidote.'

The personae are people familiar to Hardy in his childhood, here universalised into the types of the whole social spectrum known to him. The contemplation of the 'group of local hearts and heads' has been realised through local, even intimate, particulars. These characters are represented, after death, as having transcended their humanity and achieved divine status through non-attachment to earthly things. Is there not something Godlike about Hardy's poetically achieved compassion?

Indeed, it is this universal, yet particularised, compassion which to me is Hardy's greatest quality. He was very much a man of his time, and it has even been claimed that he was a product of the age of steam. It must be admitted, at any rate, that he was fascinated by railways. Many of his poems recount incidents in waiting-rooms and railway carriages, the scene of brief chance encounters—except that Hardy was not a convinced believer in chance. His mind conceived the dichotomy of chance and destiny—as much a feature of British Rail today as it was when Hardy's own destiny took him to Paddington station. The best of his railway poems is *Midnight on the Great Western* (p. 53). To these twenty lines of quintessential Hardy, no comment can have any relevance, though one might draw attention to the superbly assured diction. The final line consisits of the four words: 'But are not of'. The writer who achieved this was no journeyman. He was of Shakespeare's craft.

Like Shakespeare, Hardy had a rich sense of comedy—usually, though not always, touched with irony. The lighter side of his graveyard obsession, such as one finds in *In the Cemetery* (p. 46), and *The Levelled Churchyard* (p. 49), has often been accused of morbidity; but it seems rather in the tradition of occupational humour attributed to gravediggers from *Hamlet* onwards.

The tone of a man so deeply involved in a general problem that he cannot afford to take it quite seriously appears again in Hardy's poems of social comedy, like *The Ruined Maid* (p. 73), based on the serious issues dwelt on in the novels of Dickens, in Mayhew's *London Labour and the London Poor,* and in his own *Tess. The Ruined Maid* is beautifully poised between irony and comedy, a *tour de force* of the dialogue form which Hardy manages consummately.

A different aspect of Hardy's humour is the light but serious nostalgia with which he treats his years as a gay bachelor living in London in *Reminiscences of a Dancing man* (p. 72). His imagining of a partly autobiographical persona recalls Browning's dramatic monologues, but Hardy's touch is lighter.

In this Introduction the biographical aspect of Hardy's poetry has been left to separate treatment, but of course life and poetry interact. It is one of the most fascinating questions of literary criticism how much it is necessary to know biographical details to understand a man's writing. Hardy is explicit about the connection, and in his case the proof of its importance is the effect on his poetry of the long estrangement from his first wife Emma and of her death in 1912, which precipitated a flood of poetry of the first order. In the poems of late 1912 to 1914 Hardy returns passionately to the golden years of their courtship in Cornwall, at the same time facing squarely the tragic nature of their estrangement. As he says in one of these poems, 'Summer gave us sweets, but Autumn wrought division.'

One of the features of Hardy's poetry which has recommended it to readers of recent years is its *Englishness,* its feeling for the roots of English tradition from its medieval beginnings. This sense of continuity has had a particular appeal for such poets as Blunden, Betjeman and latterly Philip Larkin. The only uneasiness felt about his sense of Anglo-Saxon continuity has been expressed by those who, following Eliot and Pound, would have preferred to connect English poetry with Continental and classical influences (there is nothing more provincial than to accuse natives of provinciality). It is clear that, to repeat what was said earlier, every reader must have his own view of Hardy, his personal canon of what is best among those thousand poems. I will conclude by quoting Larkin's triumphant and authoritive affirmation. In a very forthright review in the *Critical Quarterly* for 1966, entitled *Wanted: good Hardy critic,* Larkin asserts that Hardy's poems have not appealed strongly to modern literary criticism. Such criticism as has been published is not very illuminating. Academic critics have leaned heavily on Leavis's dismissive assertion already quoted. Larkin, writing not as a professional critic but as an active poet, concludes:

> 'Perhaps the oddest thing about contemporary Hardy criticism is the way in which its mediocre perpetrators consider themqelves justified in patronising Hardy's poems. . . . To [them] may I trumpet the assurance that one reader at least would not wis Hardy's *Collected Poems* a single page shorter, and regards it as many times over the best body of poetic work this century has so far to show?'

BIOGRAPHICAL INTRODUCTION

by Robert Gittings

Thomas Hardy was born in Dorset on 2 June 1840 in the little hamlet of Higher Bockhampton, about three miles east of Dorchester. Although he would have liked to claim relationship with Nelson's captain, afterwards Admiral Hardy, he himself could not trace his ancestry further than his great-grandfather, John Hardy of the neighbouring small town of Puddletown, who, by tradition, had an Irish mother. This great-grandfather, together with Hardy's grandfather, father, and numerous relatives, were all local masons and bricklayers; most of the women in the family were in domestic service, including Hardy's mother. Her own mother had married 'beneath her', and Jemima Hardy was ambitious for her eldest child, encouraging him in reading and serious pursuits. His father (also Thomas), though a successful craftsman, took life more easily. From him Hardy inherited a passion for music, and from an early age went fiddle-playing with his father at country dances and entertainments.

After a short time at the village school of Lower Bockhampton, Hardy went to a small school in Dorchester, and when the master opened a fee-paying establishment, Hardy's parents paid for him to continue and learn Latin. At sixteen, he was apprenticed to a Dorchester architect, John Hicks, and met the learned, self-taught Dorset poet, William Barnes, who kept a school next door; but the chief influence at this time was a son of a Vicar of Fordington, a suburb parish of Dorchester. This man, Horatio Mosely Moule, encouraged Hardy to study Greek and read intelligent magazines, though he did not advise Hardy to enter a university.

Instead, at the age of just under 22, Hardy went in 1862 to London, with letters of introduction from Hicks to various architects. The influence of one of these led to employment as architectural assistant in the office of Arthur Blomfield, well-known in church architecture. Though a competent draughtsman, Hardy's heart lay in learning about music, painting, plays and literature, and he freqented concerts, operas, galleries, and Shakespearian performances. He also began to write poetry seriously, including many sonnets, of which only a few have survived (one is on p. 15). His poems, however, lacking the fashionable Tennysonian richness, and composed with the aid of a rhyming dictionary, were rejected by every magazine to which he sent them.

Some severe emotional stress is hinted in the finest poem of this early period, *Neutral Tones* (p. 58). At all events, in the year 1867 when he wrote this, Hardy felt obliged by ill-health to return to Dorset, and to take up employment with Hicks. He also determined to turn his experiences in London and Dorset into prose, encouraged perhaps by having had a humorous article printed. His first apprentice novel was finally rejected, but he embarked on others. A job of church-restoration for Crickmay (Hicks' successor) took him in 1870 to Cornwall, where he met and fell in love with the sister-in-law of the rector of St. Juliot, Emma Lavinia Gifford, an event celebrated in the poem *When I Set Out For Lyonnesse* (p. 95). She encouraged him to continue novel-writing, acted as his amanuensis, and, following the popular success of his fourth published novel, *Far From the Madding Crowd,* in 1874, married him. After nearly two years of uncertainty, both in life and work, as is suggested by the poem *We Sat at the Window* (p. 92), Hardy found a congenial though temporary home at Sturminster Newton in Dorset; he later referred to this as 'our happiest time'.

The truth was that Hardy, always easily susceptible to women, was equally easily disillusioned. His great novel-producing periods of the 1880s and early 1890s hint at other attractions outside marriage, or hark back to earlier loves, as in

Thoughts of Phena (p. 81), concerning his cousin Tryphena Sparks. He had finally settled, in 1885, in a house designed by himself and built by his brother Henry. This was Max Gate, a mile or so from his birthplace. He drew poetic inspiration from these early ties of place and family, and the story of his most famous novel, *Tess of the d'Urbervilles* (1891), probably derives from such sources. At the same time, the popular success of this book thrust him increasingly into London society. Since his days with Blomfield, Hardy had regarded himself as at least half a Londoner, but his social life there had been largely masculine. Now he was taken up by society ladies, especially by those who had literary ambitions. It was the death-blow to his marriage to the erratic but not untalented Emma, and twenty years of tacit estrangement ensued, revealed in such poems as *A Dead Man Walking* (p. 22).

In the late 1890s Hardy decided to abandon prose fiction, after (but not perhaps entirely on account of) the bad reception of *Jude the Obscure,* and in 1898, at the age of 58, he published his first book of poetry, *Wessex Poems,* Many dated back to the 1860s and Hardy was deeply chagrined when some critics treated the book as a new and unsuccessful experiment by one whose métier was novel-writing. His desires to prove this verdict wrong was part of the motive for his extraordinary poetic output in the last thirty years of his life. Work on his monumental epic, *The Dynasts,* occupied much of the first decade of the twentieth century, and Hardy became noticeably exhausted physically and mentally, confessing as much to close friends. The death of his much-loved mother in 1904 (his father had died in 1892) further depressed him.

About 1906, however, he met a young elementary school teacher, of Dorset descent, but living and working in Enfield, where she contributed to the children's column of the local paper. Florence Emily Dugdale was then in her late twenties, nearly 40 years younger than he, and with the type of beauty which always attracted Hardy. Obtaining a reader's ticket for the British Museum, she helped him revise the third part of *The*

Dynasts, while he attempted to further her literary ambitions by writing glowing letters of recommendation to editors and publishers. He did not for some years introduce her to his wife, and friends had to contrive occasions for Hardy and Florence to go on holiday together, without, as one wrote, 'Emma intervening'.

In the summer of 1910 Hardy had the Order of Merit conferred upon him. He also contrived that his wife and Miss Dugdale should meet. Florence had experience in caring for the elderly and pathetic—as Emma now was—and a friendship sprang up between the two women; they even went on holiday together. Emma, however, suffered from a chronic and painful illness, and died in November 1912. Instantly, Hardy was stricken by remorse, and poured out poems to his dead wife, mainly recalling their Cornish romance forty years before. He visited St. Juliot exactly 43 years after their first meeting there. His actions were painful to Florence, who found his few wistful poetic tributes to herself swamped by dozens of poems of the highest quality, inspired by his memories of Emma, and by a manuscript she had left, describing her early life and their courtship. Such poems, *After a Journey* (p. 1), *At Castle Boterel* (p. 4), *The Going* (p. 31), *The Haunter* (p. 34), *The Voice* (p. 86), and many others were published by Hardy in November 1914. Earlier that year he had married Florence Dugdale; but poems to Emma continued to be written and form a considerable body in his later publications.

Honorary doctorates (Cambridge 1913, Oxford 1920) were awarded to Hardy, and there were many other tributes in the latter year, in which he celebrated his eightieth birthday. His morbid sensitivity, allied with his depressive horror at what he considered mankind's crowning folly in the Great War, caused him generally to retire from life, particularly after the death in 1915 of his sister Mary, to whom he wrote several poems, including *Logs on the Hearth* (p. 51). He became, however, something of a cult among younger post-war poets and writers, and pilgrimages to Max Gate were made by such people as

Siegfried Sassoon, Edmund Blunden, Virginia Woolf, Robert Graves, Walter de la Mare, and Middleton Murry. To them he appeared, rightly, not a mere survivor from the nineteenth century, but a poet of their own twentieth century. His disillusion with life, which dated from his very earliest utterances, now seemed appropriate to the cynical spirit of the 1920s. His poems were favourably reviewed right up to his death, which occured at Max Gate on 11 January 1928. In a somewhat grotesque confusion of motives, his ashes were placed in Westminster Abbey, and his heart buried next to Emma in the churchyard at Stinsford, the parish where he had been born.

Hardy published eight books of poems, *Wessex Poems* (1898), *Poems of the Past and the Present* (1901), *Time's Laughingstocks* (1909), *Satires of Circumstance* (1914), *Moments of Vision* (1917), *Late Lyrics and Earlier* (1922), *Human Shows* (1925), and *Winter Words* (1928), the last-named appearing posthumously. Quietly bitter about most criticism, he could be quite violent over any reviewers who did not value his poems far above his prose, an attitude which many onlookers, such as E. M. Forster, found disturbing. This unfortunately pervaded not only some of his prefaces, but also his disguised autobiography, published after his death as the work of his second wife, and carefully written in the third person so as to seem her biography of him. His perpetual adolescence—he confessed to his second wife that he thought he had never grown up—made many of the poems of his old age seem as fresh and youthful as some of his earliest.

His personal life was full of contrasts. His frequently expressed tenderness over the sufferings of animals could exist alongside instances of extreme insensitivity to the feelings of human beings. Disclaiming any fixed philosophy, and disliking the frequent label of pessimist, his pronouncements in prose and verse often seem to strike a deliberate and provocative note of gloom. A grim humour which, he always maintained, the critics misread, appears in a poem such as *The Levelled Churchyard* (p. 49). Determinedly sceptical in thought, he maintained that if there had been a God, his own search over a long life would certainly have found one. Yet he remained what he himself called 'churchy', and echoes of Prayer Book and Bible pervade his poems, and indeed all his writing. He never quite relinquished the hope that the Church would reorganise itself in a way acceptable to those who, like himself, could not accept its conventional tenets. He was always 'hoping it might be so', in the words of his own poem *The Oxen* (p. 64).

After a Journey

Hereto I come to view a voiceless ghost;
  Whither, O whither will its whim now draw me?
Up the cliff, down, till I'm lonely, lost,
  And the unseen waters' ejaculations awe me.
Where you will next be there's no knowing,
  Facing round about me everywhere,
    With your nut-coloured hair,
And gray eyes, and rose-flush coming and going.

Yes: I have re-entered your olden haunts at last;
  Through the years, through the dead scenes I have tracked you;
What have you now found to say of our past—
  Scanned across the dark space wherein I have lacked you?
Summer gave us sweets, but autumn wrought division?
  Things were not lastly as firstly well
    With us twain, you tell?
But all's closed now, despite Time's derision.

I see what you are doing: you are leading me on
  To the spots we knew when we haunted here together,
The waterfall, above which the mist-bow shone
  At the then fair hour in the then fair weather,
And the cave just under, with a voice still so hollow
  That it seems to call out to me from forty years ago,
    When you were all aglow,
And not the thin ghost that I now frailly follow!

Ignorant of what there is flitting here to see,
  The waked birds preen and the seals flop lazily;
Soon you will have, Dear, to vanish from me,
  For the stars close their shutters and the dawn whitens hazily.

Trust me, I mind not, though Life lours,
The bringing me here; nay, bring me here again!
I am just the same as when
Our days were a joy, and our paths through flowers.

Pentargan Bay

Afternoon Service at Mellstock

(Circa 1850)

On afternoons of drowsy calm
We stood in the panelled pew,
Singing one-voiced a Tate-and-Brady psalm
To the tune of 'Cambridge New'.

We watched the elms, we watched the rooks,
The clouds upon the breeze,
Between the whiles of glancing at our books,
And swaying like the trees.

So mindless were those outpourings! –
Though I am not aware
That I have gained by subtle thought on things
Since we stood psalming there.

Afterwards

When the Present has latched its postern behind my tremulous stay,
And the May month flaps its glad green leaves like wings,
Delicate-filmed as new-spun silk, will the neighbours say,
'He was a man who used to notice such things'?

If it be in the dusk when, like an eyelid's soundless blink,
  The dewfall-hawk comes crossing the shades to alight
Upon the wind-warped upland thorn, a gazer may think,
  'To him this must have been a familiar sight.'

If I pass during some nocturnal blackness, mothy and warm,
  When the hedgehog travels furtively over the lawn,
One may say, 'He strove that such innocent creatures should
    come to no harm,
  But he could do little for them; and now he is gone.'

If, when hearing that I have been stilled at last, they stand at the
    door,
  Watching the full-starred heavens that winter sees,
Will this thought rise on those who will meet my face no more,
  'He was one who had an eye for such mysteries'?

And will any say when my bell of quittance is heard in the
    gloom,
  And a crossing breeze cuts a pause in its outrollings,
Till they rise again, as they were a new bell's boom,
  'He hears it not now, but used to notice such things'?

An August Midnight

I

A shaded lamp and a waving blind,
And the beat of a clock from a distant floor:
On this scene enter—winged, horned, and spined—
A longlegs, a moth, and a dumbledore;
While 'mid my page there idly stands
A sleepy fly, that rubs its hands. . . .

II

Thus meet we five, in this still place,
At this point of time, at this point in space.
—My guests besmear my new-penned line,
Or bang at the lamp and fall supine.
'God's humblest, they!' I muse. Yet why?
They know Earth-secrets that know not I.

Max Gate, 1899

At Castle Boterel

As I drive to the junction of lane and highway,
  And the drizzle bedrenches the waggonette,
I look behind at the fading byway,
  And see on its slope, now glistening wet,
    Distinctly yet

Myself and a girlish form benighted
  In dry March weather. We climb the road
Beside a chaise. We had just alighted
  To ease the sturdy pony's load
    When he sighed and slowed.

What we did as we climbed, and what we talked of
  Matters not much, nor to what it led,—
Something that life will not be balked of
  Without rude reason till hope is dead,
    And feeling fled.

It filled but a minute. But was there ever
  A time of such quality, since or before,
In that hill's story? To one mind never,
  Though it has been climbed, foot-swift, foot-sore,
    By thousands more.

Primaeval rocks form the road's steep border,
And much have they faced there, first and last,
Of the transitory in Earth's long order;
But what they record in colour and cast
Is—that we two passed.

And to me, though Time's unflinching rigour,
In mindless rote, has ruled from sight
The substance now, one phantom figure
Remains on the slope, as when that night
Saw us alight.

I look and see it there, shrinking, shrinking,
I look back at it amid the rain
For the very last time; for my sand is sinking,
And I shall traverse old love's domain
Never again.

March 1913

At the Word 'Farewell'

She looked like a bird from a cloud
On the clammy lawn,
Moving alone, bare-browed
In the dim of dawn.
The candles alight in the room
For my parting meal
Made all things withoutdoors loom
Strange, ghostly, unreal.

The hour itself was a ghost,
And it seemed to me then
As of chances the chance furthermost
I should see her again.

I beheld not where all was so fleet
  That a Plan of the past
Which had ruled us from birthtime to meet
  Was in working at last:

No prelude did I there perceive
  To a drama at all,
Or foreshadow what fortune might weave
  From beginnings so small;
But I rose as if quicked by a spur
  I was bound to obey,
And stepped through the casement to her
  Still alone in the gray.

'I am leaving you . . . Farewell!' I said,
  As I followed her on
By an alley bare boughs overspread;
  'I soon must be gone!'
Even then the scale might have been turned
  Against love by a feather,
—But crimson one cheek of hers burned
  When we came in together.

Autumn in King's Hintock Park

Here by the baring bough
  Raking up leaves,
Often I ponder how
  Springtime deceives,—
I, an old woman now,
  Raking up leaves.

Here in the avenue
    Raking up leaves,
Lords' ladies pass in view,
    Until one heaves
Sighs at life's russet hue,
    Raking up leaves!

Just as my shape you see
    Raking up leaves,
I saw, when fresh and free,
    Those memory weaves
Into grey ghosts by me,
    Raking up leaves.

Yet, Dear, though one may sigh,
    Raking up leaves,
New leaves will dance on high—
    Earth never grieves!—
Will not, when missed am I
    Raking up leaves.

1901

Beeny Cliff

March 1870–March 1913

I

O the opal and the sapphire of that wandering western sea,
And the woman riding high above with bright hair flapping
    free—
The woman whom I loved so, and who loyally loved me.

II

The pale mews plained below us, and the waves seemed far away
In a nether sky, engrossed in saying their ceaseless babbling say,
As we laughed light-heartedly aloft on that clear-sunned March day.

III

A little cloud then cloaked us, and there flew an irised rain,
And the Atlantic dyed its levels with a dull misfeatured stain,
And then the sun burst out again, and purples prinked the main.

IV

—Still in all its chasmal beauty bulks old Beeny to the sky,
And shall she and I not go there once again now March is nigh,
And the sweet things said in that March say anew there by and by?

V

What if still in chasmal beauty looms that wild weird western shore,
The woman now is—elsewhere—whom the ambling pony bore,
And nor knows nor cares for Beeny, and will laugh there nevermore.

Beyond the Last Lamp

(Near Tooting Common)

I

While rain, with eve in partnership,
Descended darkly, drip, drip, drip,
Beyond the last lone lamp I passed
    Walking slowly, whispering sadly,
    Two linked loiterers, wan, downcast:
Some heavy thought constrained each face,
And blinded them to time and place.

II

The pair seemed lovers, yet absorbed
In mental scenes no longer orbed
By love's young rays. Each countenance
    As it slowly, as it sadly
    Caught the lamplight's yellow glance,
Held in suspense a misery
At things which had been or might be.

III

When I retrod that watery way
Some hours beyond the droop of day,
Still I found pacing there the twain
    Just as slowly, just as sadly,
    Heedless of the night and rain.
One could but wonder who they were
And what wild woe detained them there.

IV

Though thirty years of blur and blot
Have slid since I beheld that spot,
And saw in curious converse there
  Moving slowly, moving sadly
  That mysterious tragic pair,
Its olden look may linger on—
All but the couple; they have gone.

V

Whither? Who knows, indeed. . . . And yet
To me, when nights are weird and wet,
Without those comrades there at tryst
  Creeping slowly, creeping sadly,
  That lone lane does not exist.
There they seem brooding on their pain,
And will, while such a lane remain.

Birds at Winter Nightfall

(Triolet)

Around the house the flakes fly faster,
And all the berries now are gone
From holly and cotonea-aster
Around the house. The flakes fly!—faster
Shutting indoors that crumb-outcaster
We used to see upon the lawn
Around the house. The flakes fly faster,
And all the berries now are gone!

Max Gate

A Bird-Scene at a Rural Dwelling

When the inmate stirs, the birds retire discreetly
From the window-ledge, whereon they whistled sweetly
        And on the step of the door,
        In the misty morning hoar;
    But now the dweller is up they flee
    To the crooked neighbouring codlin-tree;
And when he comes fully forth they seek the garden,
And call from the lofty costard, as pleading pardon
        For shouting so near before
        In their joy at being alive:—
Meanwhile the hammering clock within goes five.

I know a domicile of brown and green,
Where for a hundred summers there have been
Just such enactments, just such daybreaks seen.

A Broken Appointment

                        You did not come,
    And marching Time drew on, and wore me numb.—
    Yet less for loss of your dear presence there
    Than that I thus found lacking in your make
    That high compassion which can overbear
    Reluctance for pure lovingkindness' sake
    Grieved I, when, as the hope-hour stroked its sum,
                        You did not come.

You love not me,
And love alone can lend you loyalty;
—I know and knew it. But, unto the store
Of human deeds divine in all but name,
Was it not worth a little hour or more
To add yet this: Once you, a woman, came
To soothe a time-torn man; even though it be
You love not me?

The Choirmaster's Burial

He often would ask us
That, when he died,
After playing so many
To their last rest,
If out of us any
Should here abide,
And it would not task us,
We would with our lutes
Play over him
By his grave-brim
The psalm he liked best—
The one whose sense suits
'Mount Ephraim'—
And perhaps we should seem
To him, in Death's dream,
Like the seraphim.

As soon as I knew
That his spirit was gone
I thought this his due,
And spoke thereupon.

'I think,' said the vicar,
'A read service quicker
Than viols out-of-doors
In these frosts and hoars.
That old-fashioned way
Requires a fine day,
And it seems to me
It had better not be.'

Hence, that afternoon,
Though never knew he
That his wish could not be,
To get through it faster
They buried the master
Without any tune.

But 'twas said that, when
At the end of next night
The vicar looked out,
There struck on his ken
Thronged roundabout,
Where the frost was graying
The headstoned grass,
A band all in white
Like the saints in church-glass,
Singing and playing
The ancient stave
By the choirmaster's grave.

Such the tenor man told
When he had grown old.

Christmas: 1924

'Peace upon earth!' was said. We sing it,
And pay a million priests to bring it.
After two thousand years of mass
We've got as far as poison-gas.

1924

A Commonplace Day

The day is turning ghost,
And scuttles from the kalendar in fits and furtively,
To join the anonymous host
Of those that throng oblivion; ceding his place, maybe,
To one of like degree.

I part the fire-gnawed logs,
Rake forth the embers, spoil the busy flames, and lay the ends
Upon the shining dogs;
Further and further from the nooks the twilight's stride extends,
And beamless black impends.

Nothing of tiniest worth
Have I wrought, pondered, planned; no one thing asking blame or praise,
Since the pale corpse-like birth
Of this diurnal unit, bearing blanks in all its rays—
Dullest of dull-hued Days!

Wanly upon the panes
The rain slides, as have slid since morn my colourless thoughts; and yet
Here, while Day's presence wanes,
And over him the sepulchre-lid is slowly lowered and set,
He wakens my regret.

Regret—though nothing dear
That I wot of, was toward in the wide world at his prime,
Or bloomed elsewhere than here,
To die with his decease, and leave a memory sweet, sublime,
Or mark him out in Time. . . .

—Yet, maybe, in some soul,
In some spot undiscerned on sea or land, some impulse rose,
Or some intent upstole
Of that enkindling ardency from whose maturer glows
The world's amendment flows;

But which, benumbed at birth
By momentary chance or wile, has missed its hope to be
Embodied on the earth;
And undervoicings of this loss to man's futurity
May wake regret in me.

A Confession to a Friend in Trouble

Your troubles shrink not, though I feel them less
Here, far away, than when I tarried near;
I even smile old smiles—with listlessness—
Yet smiles they are, not ghastly mockeries mere.

A thought too strange to house within my brain
Haunting its outer precincts I discern:
—*That I will not show zeal again to learn*
Your griefs, and, sharing them, renew my pain. . . .

It goes, like murky bird or buccaneer
That shapes its lawless figure on the main,
And staunchness tends to banish utterly
The unseemly instinct that had lodgment here;
Yet, comrade old, can bitterer knowledge be
Than that, though banned, such instinct was in me!

1866

The Conformers

Yes we'll wed, my little fay,
And you shall write you mine,
And in a villa chastely gray
We'll house, and sleep, and dine.
But those night-screened, divine,
Stolen trysts of heretofore,
We of choice ecstasies and fine
Shall know no more.

The formal faced cohue
Will then no more upbraid
With smiting smiles and whisperings two
Who have thrown less loves in shade.
We shall no more evade
The searching light of the sun,
Our game of passion will be played,
Our dreaming done.

We shall not go in stealth
To rendezvous unknown,
But friends will ask me of your health,
And you about my own.
When we abide alone,
No leapings each to each,
But syllables in frigid tone
Of household speech.

When down to dust we glide
Men will not say askance,
As now: 'How all the country side
Rings with their mad romance!'
But as they graveward glance
Remark: 'In them we lose
A worthy pair, who helped advance
Sound parish views.'

The Convergence of the Twain

(Lines on the loss of the 'Titanic')

I

In a solitude of the sea
Deep from human vanity,
And the pride of life that planned her, stilly couches she.

II

Steel chambers, late the pyres
Of her salamandrine fires,
Cold currents thrid, and turn to rhythmic tidal lyres.

III

Over the mirrors meant
To glass the opulent
The sea-worm crawls—grotesque, slimed, dumb, indifferent.

IV

Jewels in joy designed
To ravish the sensuous mind
Lie lightless, all their sparkles bleared and black and blind.

V

Dim moon-eyed fishes near
Gaze at the gilded gear
And query: 'What does this vaingloriousness down here?' . . .

VI

Well: while was fashioning
This creature of cleaving wing,
The Immanent Will that stirs and urges everything

VII

Prepared a sinister mate
For her—so gaily great—
A Shape of Ice, for the time far and dissociate.

VIII

And as the smart ship grew
In stature, grace, and hue,
In shadowy silent distance grew the Iceberg too.

IX

Alien they seemed to be:
No mortal eye could see
The intimate welding of their later history,

X

Or sign that they were bent
By paths coincident
On being anon twin halves of one august event,

XI

Till the Spinner of the Years
Said 'Now!' And each one hears,
And consummation comes, and jars two hemispheres.

Copying Architecture in an Old Minster

(*Wimborne*)

How smartly the quarters of the hour march by
That the jack-o'-clock never forgets;
Ding-dong; and before I have traced a cusp's eye,
Or got the true twist of the ogee over,
A double ding-dong ricochetts.

Just so did he clang here before I came,
And so will he clang when I'm gone
Through the Minster's cavernous hollows—the same
Tale of hours never more to be will he deliver
To the speechless midnight and dawn!

I grow to conceive it a call to ghosts,
Whose mould lies below and around.
Yes; the next 'Come, come,' draws them out from their posts,
And they gather, and one shade appears and another,
As the eve-damps creep from the ground.

See—a Courtenay stands by his quatre-foiled tomb,
And a Duke and his Duchess near;
And one Sir Edmund in columned gloom,
And a Saxon king by the presbytery chamber;
And shapes unknown in the rear.

Maybe they have met for a parle on some plan
To better ail-stricken mankind;
I catch their cheepings, though thinner than
The overhead creak of a passager's pinion
When leaving land behind.

Or perhaps they speak to the yet unborn,
And caution them not to come
To a world so ancient and trouble-torn,
Of foiled intents, vain lovingkindness,
And ardours chilled and numb.

They waste to fog as I stir and stand,
And move from the arched recess,
And pick up the drawing that slipped from my hand,
And feel for the pencil I dropped in the cranny
In a moment's forgetfulness.

The Darkling Thrush

I leant upon a coppice gate
When Frost was spectre-gray,
And Winter's dregs made desolate
The weakening eye of day.
The tangled bine-stems scored the sky
Like strings of broken lyres,
And all mankind that haunted nigh
Had sought their household fires.

The land's sharp features seemed to be
The Century's corpse outleant,
His crypt the cloudy canopy,
The wind his death-lament.
The ancient pulse of germ and birth
Was shrunken hard and dry,
And every spirit upon earth
Seemed fervourless as I.

At once a voice arose among
The bleak twigs overhead
In a full-hearted evensong
Of joy illimited;
An aged thrush, frail, gaunt, and small,
In blast-beruffled plume,
Had chosen thus to fling his soul
Upon the growing gloom.

So little cause for carolings
Of such ecstatic sound
Was written on terrestrial things
Afar or nigh around,
That I could think there trembled through
His happy good-night air
Some blessed Hope, whereof he knew
And I was unaware.

31 December 1900

The Dead Man Walking

They hail me as one living,
But don't they know
That I have died of late years,
Untombed although?

I am but a shape that stands here,
A pulseless mould,
A pale past picture, screening
Ashes gone cold.

Not at a minute's warning,
Not in a loud hour,
For me ceased Time's enchantments
In hall and bower.

There was no tragic transit,
No catch of breath,
When silent seasons inched me
On to this death. . . .

—A Troubadour-youth I rambled
With Life for lyre,
The beats of being raging
In me like fire.

But when I practised eyeing
The goal of men,
It iced me, and I perished
A little then.

When passed my friend, my kinsfolk,
Through the Last Door,
And left me standing bleakly,
I died yet more;

And when my Love's heart kindled
In hate of me,
Wherefore I knew not, died I
One more degree.

And if when I died fully
I cannot say,
And changed into the corpse-thing
I am to-day;

Yet is it that, though whiling
The time somehow
In walking, talking smiling,
I live not now.

A Death-Day Recalled

Beeny did not quiver,
Juliot grew not gray,
Thin Vallency's river
Held its wonted way.
Bos seemed not to utter
Dimmest note of dirge,
Targan mouth a mutter
To its creamy surge.

Yet though these, unheeding,
Listless, passed the hour
Of her spirit's speeding,
She had, in her flower,
Sought and loved the places—
Much and often pined
For their lonely faces
When in towns confined.

Why did not Vallency
   In his purl deplore
One whose haunts were whence he
   Drew his limpid store?
Why did Bos not thunder,
   Targan apprehend
Body and Breath were sunder
   Of their former friend?

The Dream Is—Which?

I am laughing by the brook with her,
   Splashed in its tumbling stir;
And then it is a blankness looms
   As if I walked not there,
Nor she, but found me in haggard rooms,
   And treading a lonely stair.

With radiant cheeks and rapid eyes
   We sit where none espies;
Till a harsh change comes edging in
   As no such sense were there,
But winter, and I were bent and thin,
   And cinder-gray my hair.

We dance in heys around the hall,
   Weightless as thistleball;
And then a curtain drops between,
   As if I danced not there,
But wandered through a mounded green
   To find her, I knew where.

March 1913

Drummer Hodge

I

They throw in Drummer Hodge, to rest
    Uncoffined—just as found:
His landmark is a kopje-crest
    That breaks the veldt around;
And foreign constellations west
    Each night above his mound.

II

Young Hodge the Drummer never knew—
    Fresh from his Wessex home—
The meaning of the broad Karoo,
    The Bush, the dusty loam,
And why uprose to nightly view
    Strange stars amid the gloam.

III

Yet portion of that unknown plain
    Will Hodge for ever be;
His homely Northern breast and brain
    Grow to some Southern tree,
And strange-eyed constellations reign
    His stars eternally.

During Wind and Rain

They sing their dearest songs—
He, she, all of them—yea,
Treble and tenor and bass,
    And one to play;

With the candles mooning each face. . . .
    Ah, no; the years O!
How the sick leaves reel down in throngs!

They clear the creeping moss—
Elders and juniors—aye,
Making the pathways neat
    And the garden gay;
And they build a shady seat. . . .
    Ah, no; the years, the years;
See, the white storm-birds wing across!

They are blithely breakfasting all—
Men and maidens—yea,
Under the summer tree,
    With a glimpse of the bay,
While pet fowl come to the knee. . . .
    Ah, no; the years O!
And the rotten rose is ript from the wall.

They change to a high new house;
He, she, all of them—aye,
Clocks and carpets and chairs
    On the lawn all day,
And brightest things that are theirs. . . .
    Ah, no; the years, the years;
Down their carved names the rain-drop ploughs.

The Eve of Waterloo

(Chorus of Phantoms)

The eyelids of eve fall together at last,
And the forms so foreign to field and tree
Lie down as though native, and slumber fast!

Sore are the thrills of misgivings we see
In the artless champaign at this harlequinade,
Distracting a vigil where calm should be!

The green seems opprest, and the Plain afraid
Of a Something to come, whereof these are the proofs,—
Neither earthquake, nor storm, nor eclipse's shade!

Yea, the coneys are scared by the thud of hoofs,
And their white scuts flash at their vanishing heels,
And swallows abandon the hamlet-roofs.

The mole's tunnelled chambers are crushed by wheels,
The lark's eggs scattered, their owners fled;
And the hedgehog's household the sapper unseals.

The snail draws in at the terrible tread,
But in vain; he is crushed by the felloe-rim;
The worm asks what can be overhead,

And wriggles deep from a scene so grim,
And guesses him safe; for he does not know
What a foul red flood will be soaking him!

Beaten about by the heel and toe
Are butterflies, sick of the day's long rheum,
To die of a worse than the weather-foe.

Trodden and bruised to a miry tomb
Are ears that have greened but will never be gold,
And flowers in the bud that will never bloom.

So the season's intent, ere its fruit unfold,
Is frustrate, and mangled, and made succumb,
Like a youth of promise struck stark and cold! . . .

And what of these who to-night have come?
—The young sleep sound; but the weather awakes
In the veterans, pains from the past that numb;

Old stabs of Ind, old Peninsular aches,
Old Friedland chills, haunt their moist mud bed,
Cramps from Austerlitz; till their slumber breaks.

And each soul shivers as sinks his head
On the loam he's to lease with the other dead
From tomorrow's mist-fall till Time be sped!

From 'The Dynasts'

The Five Students

The sparrow dips in his wheel-rut bath,
The sun grows passionate-eyed,
And boils the dew to smoke by the paddock-path;
As strenuously we stride,—
Five of us; dark He, fair He, dark She, fair She, I,
All beating by.

The air is shaken, the high-road hot,
Shadowless swoons the day,
The greens are sobered and cattle at rest; but not
We on our urgent way,—
Four of us; fair She, dark She, fair He, I, are there,
But one—elsewhere.

Autumn moulds the hard fruit mellow,
And forward still we press
Through moors, briar-meshed plantations, clay-pits yellow,
As in the spring hours—yes,
Three of us; fair He, fair She, I, as heretofore,
But—fallen one more.

The leaf drops: earthworms draw it in
At night-time noiselessly,
The fingers of birch and beech are skeleton-thin,
And yet on the beat are we,—
Two of us; fair She, I. But no more left to go
The track we know.

Icicles tag the church-aisle leads,
The flag-rope gibbers hoarse,
The home-bound foot-folk wrap their snow-flaked heads,
Yet I still stalk the course—
One of us. . . . Dark and fair He, dark and fair She, gone:
The rest—anon.

Friends Beyond

William Dewy, Tranter Reuben, Farmer Ledlow late at plough,
Robert's kin, and John's, and Ned's,
And the Squire, and Lady Susan, lie in Mellstock churchyard now!

'Gone,' I call them, gone for good, that group of local hearts and heads;
Yet at mothy curfew-tide,
And at midnight when the noon-heat breathes it back from walls and leads,

They've a way of whispering to me—fellow-wight who yet abide—
In the muted, measured note
Of a ripple under archways, or a lone cave's stillicide:

'We have triumphed: this achievement turns the bane to antidote,
Unsuccesses to success,
Many thought-worn eves and morrows to a morrow free of thought.

'No more need we corn and clothing, feel of old terrestrial stress;
Chill detraction stirs no sigh;
Fear of death has even bygone us: death gave all that we possess.'

W.D.—'Ye mid burn the old bass-viol that I set such value by.'
Squire.—'You may hold the manse in fee,
You may wed my spouse, may let my children's memory of me die.'

Lady S.—'You may have my rich brocades, my laces; take each household key;
Ransack coffer, desk, bureau;
Quiz the few poor treasures hid there, con the letters kept by me.'

Far.—'Ye mid zell my favourite heifer, ye mid let the charlock grow,
Foul the grinterns, give up thrift.'
Far. Wife.—'If ye break my best blue china, children, I shan't care or ho.'
All.—'We've no wish to hear the tidings, how the people's fortunes shift;
What your daily doings are;
Who are wedded, born, divided; if your lives beat slow or swift.

'Curious not the least are we if our intents you make or mar,
If you quire to our old tune,
If the City stage still passes, if the weirs still roar afar.'

—Thus, with very gods' composure, freed those crosses late and soon
Which, in life, the Trine allow
(Why none witteth), and ignoring all that haps beneath the moon,

William Dewy, Tranter Reuben, Farmer Ledlow late at plough,
Robert's kin, and John's, and Ned's,
And the Squire, and Lady Susan, murmur mildly to me now.

The Going

Why did you give no hint that night
That quickly after the morrow's dawn,
And calmly, as if indifferent quite,
You would close your term here, up and be gone
Where I could not follow
With wing of swallow
To gain one glimpse of you ever anon!

Never to bid good-bye,
Or lip me the softest call,
Or utter a wish for a word, while I
Saw morning harden upon the wall,
Unmoved, unknowing
That your great going
Had place that moment, and altered all.

Why do you make me leave the house
And think for a breath it is you I see
At the end of the alley of bending boughs
Where so often at dusk you used to be;
Till in darkening dankness
The yawning blankness
Of the perspective sickens me!

You were she who abode
By those red-veined rocks far West,
You were the swan-necked one who rode
Along the beetling Beeny Crest,

And, reining nigh me,
Would muse and eye me,
While Life unrolled us its very best.

Why, then, latterly did we not speak,
Did we not think of those days long dead,
And ere your vanishing strive to seek
That time's renewal? We might have said,
'In this bright spring weather
We'll visit together
Those places that once we visited.'

Well, well! All's past amend,
Unchangeable. It must go.
I seem but a dead man held on end
To sink down soon. . . . O you could not know
That such swift fleeing
No soul foreseeing—
Not even I—would undo me so!

December 1912

Great Things

Sweet cyder is a great thing,
A great thing to me,
Spinning down to Weymouth town
By Ridgway thirstily,
And maid and mistress summoning
Who tend the hostelry:
O cyder is a great thing,
A great thing to me!

The dance it is a great thing,
  A great thing to me,
With candles lit and partners fit
  For night-long revelry;
And going home when day-dawning
  Peeps pale upon the lea:
O dancing is a great thing,
  A great thing to me!

Love is, yea, a great thing,
  A great thing to me,
When, having drawn across the lawn
  In darkness silently,
A figure flits like one a-wing
  Out from the nearest tree:
O love is, yes, a great thing,
  A great thing to me!

Will these be always great things,
  Great things to me? . . .
Let it befall that One will call,
  'Soul, I have need of thee:'
What then? Joy-jaunts, impassioned flings,
  Love, and its ecstasy,
Will always have been great things,
  Great things to me!

Green Slates

(Penpethy)

It happened once, before the duller
  Loomings of life defined them,
I searched for slates of greenish colour
  A quarry where men mined them;

And saw, the while I peered around there,
In the quarry standing
A form against the slate background there,
Of fairness eye-commanding.

And now, though fifty years have flown me,
With all their dreams and duties,
And strange-pipped dice my hand has thrown me,
And dust are all her beauties,

Green slates—seen high on roofs, or lower
In waggon, truck or lorry—
Cry out: 'Our home was where you saw her
Standing in the quarry!'

The Haunter

He does not think that I haunt here nightly:
How shall I let him know
That whither his fancy sets him wandering
I, too, alertly go?—
Hover and hover a few feet from him
Just as I used to do,
But cannot answer the words he lifts me—
Only listen thereto!

When I could answer he did not say them:
When I could let him know
How I would like to join in his journeys
Seldom he wished to go.
Now that he goes and he wants me with him
More than he used to do,
Never he sees my faithful phantom
Though he speaks thereto.

Yes, I companion him to places
Only dreamers know,
Where the shy hares print long paces,
Where the night rooks go;
Into old aisles where the past is all to him,
Close as his shade can do,
Always lacking the power to call to him,
Near as I reach thereto!

What a good haunter I am, O tell him!
Quickly make him know
If he but sigh since my loss befell him
Straight to his side I go.
Tell him a faithful one is doing
All that love can do
Still that his path may be worth pursuing,
And to bring peace thereto.

Her Dilemma

(In —— Church)

The two were silent in a sunless church,
Whose mildewed walls, uneven paving-stones,
And wasted carvings passed antique research;
And nothing broke the clock's dull monotones.

Leaning against a wormy poppy-head,
So wan and worn that he could scarcely stand,
—For he was soon to die,—he softly said,
'Tell me you love me!'—holding long her hand.

She would have given a world to breathe 'yes' truly,
So much his life seemed hanging on her mind,
And hence she lied, her heart persuaded throughly
'Twas worth her soul to be a moment kind.

But the sad need thereof, his nearing death,
So mocked humanity that she shamed to prize
A world conditioned thus, or care for breath
Where Nature such dilemmas could devise.

1866

Heredity

I am the family face;
Flesh perishes, I live on,
Projecting trait and trace
Through time to times anon,
And leaping from place to place
Over oblivion.

The years-heired feature that can
In curve and voice and eye
Despise the human span
Of durance—that is I;
The eternal thing in man,
That heeds no call to die.

Horses Aboard

Horses in horsecloths stand in a row
On board the huge ship that at last lets go:
Whither are they sailing? They do not know,
Nor what for, nor how.—
They are horses of war,
And are going to where there is fighting afar;
But they gaze through their eye-holes unwitting they are,
And that in some wilderness, gaunt and ghast,
Their bones will bleach ere a year has passed,
And the item be as 'war-waste' classed.—
And when the band booms, and the folk say 'Good-bye!'
And the shore slides astern, they appear wrenched awry
From the scheme Nature planned for them,—wondering why.

The House of Hospitalities

Here we broached the Christmas barrel,
  Pushed up the charred log-ends;
Here we sang the Christmas carol,
    And called in friends.

Time has tired me since we met here
  When the folk now dead were young,
Since the viands were outset here
    And quaint songs sung.

And the worm has bored the viol
  That used to lead the tune,
Rust eaten out the dial
    That struck night's noon.

Now no Christmas brings in neighbours,
  And the new year comes unlit;
Where we sang the mole now labours,
    And spiders knit.

Yet at midnight if here walking,
  When the moon sheets wall and tree,
I see forms of old time talking,
    Who smile on me.

I Am the One

I am the one whom ringdoves see
    Through chinks in boughs
    When they do not rouse
    In sudden dread,
But stay on cooing, as if they said:
    'Oh; it's only he.'

I am the passer when up-eared hares,
Stirred as they eat
The new-sprung wheat,
Their munch resume
As if they thought: 'He is one for whom
Nobody cares.'

Wet-eyed mourners glance at me
As in train they pass
Along the grass
To a hollowed spot,
And think: 'No matter; he quizzes not
Our misery.'

I hear above: 'We stars must lend
No fierce regard
To his gaze, so hard
Bent on us thus,—
Must scathe him not. He is one with us
Beginning and end.'

I Found Her Out There

I found her out there
On a slope few see,
That falls westwardly
To the salt-edged air,
Where the ocean breaks
On the purple strand,
And the hurricane shakes
The solid land.

I brought her here,
And have laid her to rest
In a noiseless nest
No sea beats near.
She will never be stirred
In her loamy cell
By the waves long heard
And loved so well.

So she does not sleep
By those haunted heights
The Atlantic smites
And the blind gales sweep,
Whence she often would gaze
At Dundagel's famed head,
While the dipping blaze
Dyed her face fire-red;

And would sigh at the tale
Of sunk Lyonnesse,
As a wind-tugged tress
Flapped her cheek like a flail;
Or listen at whiles
With a thought-bound brow
To the murmuring miles
She is far from now.

Yet her shade, maybe,
Will creep underground
Till it catch the sound
Of that western sea
As it swells and sobs
Where she once domiciled,
And joy in its throbs
With the heart of a child.

I Have Lived with Shades

I

I have lived with Shades so long,
And talked to them so oft,
Since forth from cot and croft
I went mankind among,
    That sometimes they
    In their dim style
    Will pause awhile
    To hear my say;

II

And take me by the hand,
And lead me through their rooms
In the To-be, where Dooms
Half-wove and shapeless stand:
    And show from there
    The dwindled dust
    And rot and rust
    Of things that were.

III

'Now turn,' they said to me
One day: 'Look whence we came,
And signify his name
Who gazes thence at thee.'—
    —'Nor name nor race
    Know I, or can,'
    I said, 'Of man
    So commonplace.

IV

'He moves me not at all;
I note no ray or jot
Of rareness in his lot,
Or star exceptional.
Into the dim
Dead throngs around
He'll sink, nor sound
Be left of him.'

V

'Yet,' said they, 'his frail speech,
Hath accents pitched like thine—
Thy mould and his define
A likeness each to each—
But go! Deep pain
Alas, would be
His name to thee,
And told in vain!'

2 February 1899

I Look Into My Glass

I look into my glass,
And view my wasting skin,
And say, 'Would God it came to pass
My heart had shrunk as thin!'

For then, I, undistrest
By hearts grown cold to me,
Could lonely wait my endless rest
With equanimity.

But Time, to make me grieve,
Part steals, lets part abide;
And shakes this fragile frame at eve
With throbbings of noontide.

The Impercipient

(At a Cathedral Service)

That with this bright believing band
I have no claim to be,
That faiths by which my comrades stand
Seem fantasies to me,
And mirage-mists their Shining Land,
Is a strange destiny.

Why thus my soul should be consigned
To infelicity,
Why always I must feel as blind
To sights my brethren see,
Why joys they've found I cannot find,
Abides a mystery.

Since heart of mine knows not that ease
Which they know; since it be
That He who breathes All's Well to these
Breathes no All's-Well to me,
My lack might move their sympathies
And Christian charity!

I am like a gazer who should mark
An inland company
Standing upfingered, with, 'Hark! hark!
The glorious distant sea!'
And feel, 'Alas, 'tis but yon dark
And wind-swept pine to me!'

Yet I would bear my shortcomings
With meet tranquillity,
But for the charge that blessed things
I'd liefer not have be,
O, doth a bird deprived of wings
Go earth-bound wilfully!

. . .

Enough. As yet disquiet clings
About us. Rest shall we.

In a Waiting Room

On a morning sick as the day of doom
With the drizzling gray
Of an English May,
There were few in the railway waiting-room.
Above its walls were framed and varnished
Pictures of liners, fly-brown, tarnished.
The table bore a Testament
For travellers' reading, if suchwise bent.

I read it on and on,
And, thronging the Gospel of Saint John,
Were figures—additions, multiplications—
By some one scrawled, with sundry emendations;
Not scoffingly designed,
But with an absent mind,—
Plainly a bagman's counts of cost,
What he had profited, what lost;
And whilst I wondered if there could have been
Any particle of a soul
In that poor man at all,
To cypher rates of wage
Upon that printed page,
There joined in the charmless scene

And stood over me and the scribbled book
(To lend the hour's mean hue
A smear of tragedy too)
A soldier and a wife, with haggard look
Subdued to stone by strong endeavour;
And then I heard
From a casual word
They were parting as they believed for ever.

But next there came
Like the eastern flame
Of some high altar, children—a pair—
Who laughed at the fly-blown pictures there.
'Here are the lovely ships that we,
Mother, are by and by going to see!
When we get there it's most sure to be fine,
And the band will play, and the sun will shine!'

It rained on the skylight with a din
As we waited and still no train came in;
But the words of the child in the squalid room
Had spread a glory through the gloom.

In Church

'And now to God the Father,' he ends,
And his voice thrills up to the topmost tiles:
Each listener chokes as he bows and bends,
And emotion pervades the crowded aisles.
Then the preacher glides to the vestry-door,
And shuts it, and thinks he is seen no more.

The door swings softly ajar meanwhile,
And a pupil of his in the Bible class,
Who adores him as one without gloss or guile,
Sees her idol stand with a satisfied smile
And re-enact at the vestry-glass
Each pulpit gesture in deft dumb-show
That had moved the congregation so.

In the British Museum

'What do you see in that time-touched stone,
        When nothing is there
But ashen blankness, although you give it
        A rigid stare?

'You look not quite as if you saw,
        But as if you heard,
Parting your lips, and treading softly
        As mouse or bird.

'It is only the base of a pillar, they'll tell you,
        That came to us
From a far old hill men used to name
        Areopagus.'

—'I know no art, and I only view
        A stone from a wall,
But I am thinking that stone has echoed
        The voice of Paul,

'Paul as he stood and preached beside it
        Facing the crowd,
A small gaunt figure with wasted features,
        Calling out loud

'Words that in all their intimate accents
Patterned upon
That marbled front, and were wide reflected,
And then were gone.

'I'm a labouring man, and know but little,
Or nothing at all;
But I can't help thinking that stone once echoed
The voice of Paul.'

In the Cemetery

'You see those mothers squabbling there?'
Remarks the man of the cemetery.
'One says in tears, *"'Tis mine lies here!"*
Another, *"Nay, mine, you Pharisee!"*
Another, *"How dare you move my flowers*
And put your own on this grave of ours!"
But all their children were laid therein
At different times, like sprats in a tin.

'And then the main drain had to cross,
And we moved the lot some nights ago,
And packed them away in the general foss
With hundreds more. But their folks don't know,
And as well cry over a new-laid drain
As anything else, to ease your pain!'

In Time of 'The Breaking of Nations'

I

Only a man harrowing clods
  In a slow silent walk
With an old horse that stumbles and nods
  Half asleep as they stalk.

II

Only thin smoke without flame
  From the heaps of couch-grass;
Yet this will go onward the same
  Though Dynasties pass.

III

Yonder a maid and her wight
  Come whispering by:
War's annals will cloud into night
  Ere their story die.

1915

Lament

How she would have loved
A party to-day!—
Bright-hatted and gloved,
With table and tray
And chairs on the lawn
Her smiles would have shone
With welcomings. . . . But
She is shut, she is shut
    From friendship's spell
    In the jailing shell
    Of her tiny cell.

Or she would have reigned
At a dinner to-night
With ardours unfeigned,
And a generous delight;
All in her abode
She'd have freely bestowed
On her guests. . . . But alas,
She is shut under grass
        Where no cups flow,
        Powerless to know
        That it might be so.

And she would have sought
With a child's eager glance
The shy snowdrops brought
By the new year's advance,
And peered in the rime
Of Candlemas-time
For crocuses . . . chanced
It that she were not tranced
        From sights she loved best;
        Wholly possessed
        By an infinite rest!

And we are here staying
Amid these stale things,
Who care not for gaying,
And those junketings
That used so to joy her,
And never to cloy her
As us they cloy! . . . But
She is shut, she is shut
        From the cheer of them, dead
        To all done and said
        In her yew-arched bed.

The Later Autumn

Gone are the lovers, under the bush
Stretched at their ease;
Gone the bees,
Tangling themselves in your hair as they rush
On the line of your track,
Leg-laden, back
With a dip to their hive
In a prepossessed dive.

Toadsmeat is mangy, frosted, and sere;
Apples in grass
Crunch as we pass,
And rot ere the men who make cyder appear.
Couch-fires abound
On fallows around,
And shades far extend
Like lives soon to end.

Spinning leaves join the remains shrunk and brown
Of last year's display
That lie wasting away,
On whose corpses they earlier as scorners gazed down
From their aery green height:
Now in the same plight
They huddle; while yon
A robin looks on.

The Levelled Churchyard

'O Passenger, pray list and catch
Our sighs and piteous groans,
Half stifled in this jumbled patch
Of wrenched memorial stones!

'We late-lamented, resting here,
Are mixed to human jam,
And each to each exclaims in fear,
"I know not which I am!"

'The wicked people have annexed
The verses on the good;
A roaring drunkard sports the text
Teetotal Tommy should!

'Where we are huddled none can trace,
And if our names remain,
They pave some path or porch or place
Where we have never lain!

'Here's not a modest maiden elf
But dreads the final Trumpet,
Lest half of her should rise herself,
And half some sturdy strumpet!

'From restorations of Thy fane,
From smoothings of Thy sward,
From zealous Churchmen's pick and plane
Deliver us O Lord! Amen!'

1882

Life and Death at Sunrise

(Near Dogbury Gate, 1867)

The hills uncap their tops
Of woodland, pasture, copse,
And look on the layers of mist
At their foot that still persist:
They are like awakened sleepers on one elbow lifted,
Who gaze around to learn if things during night have shifted.

A waggon creaks up from the fog
With a laboured leisurely jog;
Then a horseman from off the hill-tip
Comes clapping down into the dip;
While woodlarks, finches, sparrows, try to entune at one time,
And cocks and hens and cows and bulls take up the chime.

With a shouldered basket and flagon
A man meets the one with the waggon,
And both the men halt of long use.
'Well,' the waggoner says, 'what's the news?'
'—'Tis a boy this time. You've just met the doctor trotting back.
She's doing very well. And we think we shall call him "Jack".

'And what have you got covered there?'
He nods to the waggon and mare.
'Oh, a coffin for old John Thinn:
We are just going to put him in.'
'—So he's gone at last. He always had a good constitution.'
'—He was ninety-odd. He could call up the French Revolution.'

Logs on the Hearth

A Memory of a Sister

The fire advances along the log
Of the tree we felled,
Which bloomed and bore striped apples by the peck
Till its last hour of bearing knelled.

The fork that first my hand would reach
And then my foot
In climbings upward inch by inch, lies now
Sawn, sapless, darkening with soot.

Where the bark chars is where, one year,
It was pruned, and bled—
Then overgrew the wound. But now, at last,
Its growings all have stagnated.

My fellow-climber rises dim
From her chilly grave—
Just as she was, her foot near mine on the bending limb,
Laughing, her young brown hand awave.

December 1915

Men Who March Away

(Song of the Soldiers)

What of the faith and fire within us
Men who march away
Ere the barn-cocks say
Night is growing gray,
Leaving all that here can win us;
What of the faith and fire within us
Men who march away?

Is it a purblind prank, O think you,
Friend with the musing eye,
Who watch us stepping by
With doubt and dolorous sigh?
Can much pondering so hoodwink you!
Is it a purblind prank, O think you,
Friend with the musing eye?

Nay. We well see what we are doing,
Though some may not see—
Dalliers as they be—
England's need are we;
Her distress would leave us rueing:
Nay. We well see what we are doing,
Though some may not see!

In our heart of hearts believing
Victory crowns the just,
And that braggarts must
Surely bite the dust,
Press we to the field ungrieving,
In our heart of hearts believing
Victory crowns the just.

Hence the faith and fire within us
Men who march away
Ere the barn-cocks say
Night is growing gray,
Leaving all that here can win us;
Hence the faith and fire within us
Men who march away.

5 September 1914

Midnight on the Great Western

In the third-class seat sat the journeying boy,
And the roof-lamp's oily flame
Played down on his listless form and face,
Bewrapt past knowing to what he was going,
Or whence he came.

In the band of his hat the journeying boy
Had a ticket stuck; and a string
Around his neck bore the key of his box,
That twinkled gleams of the lamp's sad beams
Like a living thing.

What past can be yours, O journeying boy
Towards a world unknown,
Who calmly, as if incurious quite
On all at stake, can undertake
This plunge alone?

Knows your soul a sphere, O journeying boy,
Our rude realms far above,
Whence with spacious vision you mark and mete
This region of sin that you find you in,
But are not of?

The Missed Train

How I was caught
Hieing home, after days of allure,
And forced to an inn—small, obscure—
At the junction, gloom-fraught.

How civil my face
To get them to chamber me there—
A roof I had scorned, scarce aware
That it stood at the place.

And how all the night
I had dreams of the unwitting cause
Of my lodgment. How lonely I was;
How consoled by her sprite!

Thus onetime to me . . .
Dim wastes of dead years bar away
Then from now. But such happenings to-day
Fall to lovers, may be!

Years, years as shoaled seas,
Truly, stretch now between! Less and less
Shrink the visions then vast in me.—Yes,
Then in me: Now in these.

Molly Gone

No more summer for Molly and me;
  There is snow on the tree,
And the blackbirds plump large as the rooks are, almost,
  And the water is hard
Where they used to dip bills at the dawn ere her figure was lost
  To these coasts, now my prison close-barred.

No more planting by Molly and me
  Where the beds used to be
Of sweet-william; no training the clambering rose
  By the framework of fir
Now bowering the pathway, whereon it swings gaily and blows
  As if calling commendment from her.

No more jauntings by Molly and me
  To the town by the sea,
Or along over Whitesheet to Wynyard's green Gap,
  Catching Montacute Crest
To the right against Sedgmoor, and Corton-Hill's far-distant cap,
  And Pilsdon and Lewsdon to west.

No more singing by Molly to me
  In the evenings when she
Was in mood and in voice, and the candles were lit,
  And past the porch-quoin
The rays would spring out on the laurels; and dumbledores hit
  On the pane, as if wishing to join.

Where, then, is Molly, who's no more with me?
  —As I stand on this lea,
Thinking thus, there's a many-flamed star in the air,
  That tosses a sign
That her glance is regarding its face from her home, so that there
  Her eyes may have meetings with mine.

Nature's Questioning

When I look forth at dawning, pool,
Field, flock, and lonely tree,
All seem to gaze at me
Like chastened children sitting silent in a school;

Their faces dulled, constrained, and worn,
As though the master's ways
Through the long teaching days
Had cowed them till their early zest was overborne.

Upon them stirs in lippings mere
(As if once clear in call,
But now scarce breathed at all)—
'We wonder, ever wonder, why we find us here!

'Has some Vast Imbecility,
Mighty to build and blend,
But impotent to tend,
Framed us in jest, and left us now to hazardry?

'Or come we of an Automaton
Unconscious of our pains? . . .
Or are we live remains
Of Godhead dying downwards, brain and eye now gone?

'Or is it that some high Plan betides,
As yet not understood,
Of Evil stormed by Good,
We the Forlorn Hope over which Achievement strides?'

Thus things around. No answer I. . ..
Meanwhile the winds, and rains,
And Earth's old glooms and pains
Are still the same, and Life and Death are neighbours nigh.

Near Lanivet, 1872

There was a stunted handpost just on the crest,
    Only a few feet high:
She was tired, and we stopped in the twilight-time for her rest,
    At the crossways close thereby.

She leant back, being so weary, against its stem,
    And laid her arms on its own,
Each open palm stretched out to each end of them,
    Her sad face sideways thrown.

Her white-clothed form at this dim-lit cease of day
    Made her look as one crucified
In my gaze at her from the midst of the dusty way,
    And hurriedly 'Don't,' I cried.

I do not think she heard. Loosing thence she said,
    As she stepped forth ready to go,
'I am rested now.—Something strange came into my head;
    I wish I had not leant so!'

And wordless we moved onward down from the hill
    In the west cloud's murked obscure,
And looking back we could see the handpost still
    In the solitude of the moor.

'It struck her too,' I thought, for as if afraid
    She heavily breathed as we trailed;
Till she said, 'I did not think how 'twould look in the shade,
    When I leant there like one nailed.'

I, lightly: 'There's nothing in it. For *you*, anyhow!'
    —'O I know there is not,' said she . . .
'Yet I wonder. . . . If no one is bodily crucified now,
    In spirit one may be!'

And we dragged on and on, while we seemed to see
    In the running of Time's far glass
Her crucified, as she had wondered if she might be
    Some day.—Alas, alas!

Neutral Tones

We stood by a pond that winter day,
And the sun was white, as though chidden of God,
And a few leaves lay on the starving sod;
        —They had fallen from an ash, and were gray.

Your eyes on me were as eyes that rove
Over tedious riddles of years ago;
And some words played between us to and fro
        On which lost the more by our love.

The smile on your mouth was the deadest thing
Alive enough to have strength to die;
And a grin of bitterness swept thereby
        Like an ominous bird a-wing. . . .

Since then, keen lessons that love deceives,
And wrings with wrong, have shaped to me
Your face, and the God-curst sun, and a tree,
        And a pond edged with grayish leaves.

1867

The Night of Trafalgar

(Boatman's Song)

I

In the wild October night-time, when the wind raved round the
land,
And the Back-sea met the Front-sea, and our doors were
blocked with sand,
And we heard the drub of Dead-man's Bay, where bones of
thousands are,
We knew not what the day had done for us at Trafalgár.
Had done,
Had done,
For us at Trafalgár!

II

'Pull hard, and make the Nothe, or down we go!' one says, says
he.
We pulled; and bedtime brought the storm; but snug at home
slept we.
Yet all the while our gallants after fighting through the day,
Were beating up and down the dark, sou'-west of Cadiz Bay.
The dark,
The dark,
Sou'-west of Cadiz Bay!

III

The victors and the vanquished then the storm it tossed and tore,
As hard they strove, those worn-out men, upon that surly shore;
Dead Nelson and his half-dead crew, his foes from near and far,
Were rolled together on the deep that night at Trafalgár!
The deep,
The deep,
That night at Trafalgár!

From 'The Dynasts'

A Night in November

I marked when the weather changed,
And the panes began to quake,
And the winds rose up and ranged,
That night, lying half-awake.

Dead leaves blew into my room,
And alighted upon my bed,
And a tree declared to the gloom
Its sorrow that they were shed.

One leaf of them touched my hand,
And I thought that it was you
There stood as you used to stand,
And saying at last you knew!

(?) 1913

Nobody Comes

Tree-leaves labour up and down,
And through them the fainting light
Succumbs to the crawl of night.
Outside in the road the telegraph wire
To the town from the darkening land
Intones to travellers like a spectral lyre
Swept by a spectral hand.

A car comes up, with lamps full-glare,
That flash upon a tree:
It has nothing to do with me,
And whangs along in a world of its own,
Leaving a blacker air;
And mute by the gate I stand again alone,
And nobody pulls up there.

9 October 1924

No Buyers

A Street Scene

A load of brushes and baskets and cradles and chairs
Labours along the street in the rain:
With a man, a woman, a pony with whiteybrown hairs.—
The man foots in front of the horse with a shambling sway
At a slower tread than a funeral train,
While to a dirge-like tune he chants his wares,
Swinging a Turk's-head brush (in a drum-major's way
When the bandsmen march and play).

A yard from the back of the man is the whiteybrown pony's
nose:
He mirrors his master in every item of pace and pose:
He stops when the man stops, without being told,
And seems to be eased by a pause; too plainly he's old,
Indeed, not strength enough shows
To steer the disjointed waggon straight,
Which wriggles left and right in a rambling line,
Deflected thus by its own warp and weight,
And pushing the pony with it in each incline.

The woman walks on the pavement verge,
Parallel to the man:
She wears an apron white and wide in span,
And carries a like Turk's-head, but more in nursing-wise:
Now and then she joins in his dirge,
But as if her thoughts were on distant things.
The rain clams her apron till it clings. –
So, step by step, they move with their merchandize,
And nobody buys.

Not Only I

Not only I
Am doomed awhile to lie
In this close bin with earthen sides;
But the things I thought, and the songs I sang,
And the hopes I had, and the passioned pang
For people I knew
Who passed before me,
Whose memory barely abides;
And the visions I drew
That daily upbore me!

And the joyous springs and summers,
And the jaunts with blithe newcomers,
And my plans and appearances; drives and rides
That fanned my face to a lively red;
And the grays and blues
Of the far-off views,
That nobody else discerned outspread;
And little achievements for blame or praise;
Things left undone; things left unsaid;
In brief, my days!

Compressed here in six feet by two,
In secrecy
To lie with me
Till the Call shall be,
Are all these things I knew,
Which cannot be handed on;
Strange happenings quite unrecorded,
Lost to the world and disregarded,
That only thinks: 'Here moulders till Doom's-dawn
A woman's skeleton.'

Old Furniture

I know not how it may be with others
    Who sit amid relics of householdry
That date from the days of their mothers' mothers,
    But well I know how it is with me
        Continually.

I see the hands of the generations
    That owned each shiny familiar thing
In play on its knobs and indentations,
    And with its ancient fashioning
        Still dallying:

Hands behind hands, growing paler and paler,
    As in a mirror a candle-flame
Shows images of itself, each frailer
    As it recedes, though the eye may frame
        Its shape the same.

On the clock's dull dial a foggy finger,
    Moving to set the minutes right
With tentative touches that lift and linger
    In the wont of a moth on a summer night,
        Creeps to my sight.

On this old viol, too, fingers are dancing—
    As whilom—just over the strings by the nut,
The tip of a bow receding, advancing
    In airy quivers, as if it would cut
        The plaintive gut.

And I see a face by that box for tinder,
    Glowing forth in fits from the dark,
And fading again, as the linten cinder
    Kindles to red at the flinty spark,
        Or goes out stark.

Well, well. It is best to be up and doing,
    The world has no use for one to-day
Who eyes things thus—no aim pursuing!
    He should not continue in this stay,
        But sink away.

On a Midsummer Eve

I idly cut a parsley stalk,
And blew therein towards the moon;
I had not thought what ghosts would walk
With shivering footsteps to my tune.

I went, and knelt, and scooped my hand
As if to drink, into the brook,
And a faint figure seemed to stand
Above me, with the bygone look.

I lipped rough rhymes of chance, not choice,
I thought not what my words might be;
There came into my ear a voice
That turned a tenderer verse for me.

The Oxen

Christmas Eve, and twelve of the clock.
    'Now they are all on their knees,'
An elder said as we sat in a flock
    By the embers in hearthside ease.

We pictured the meek mild creatures where
    They dwelt in their strawy pen,
Nor did it occur to one of us there
    To doubt they were kneeling then.

So fair a fancy few would weave
In these years! Yet, I feel,
If someone said on Christmas Eve,
'Come; see the oxen kneel

'In the lonely barton by yonder coomb
Our childhood used to know,'
I should go with him in the gloom,
Hoping it might be so.

1915

Paths of Former Time

No; no;
It must not be so:
They are the ways we do not go.

Still chew
The kine, and moo
In the meadows we used to wander through;

Still purl
The rivulets and curl
Towards the weirs with a musical swirl;

Haymakers
As in former years
Rake rolls into heaps that the pitchfork rears;

Wheels crack
On the turfy track
The waggon pursues with its toppling pack.

'Why then shun—
Since summer's not done—
All this because of the lack of one?'

Had you been
Sharer of that scene
You would not ask while it bites in keen

Why is it so
We can no more go
By the summer paths we used to know!

1913

Paying Calls

I went by footpath and by stile
Beyond where bustle ends,
Strayed here a mile and there a mile
And called upon some friends.

On certain ones I had not seen
For years past did I call,
And then on others who had been
The oldest friends of all.

It was the time of midsummer
When they had used to roam;
But now, though tempting was the air,
I found them all at home.

I spoke to one and other of them
By mound and stone and tree
Of things we had done ere days were dim,
But they spoke not to me.

The Phantom Horsewoman

I

Queer are the ways of a man I know:
He comes and stands
In a careworn craze,
And looks at the sands
And the seaward haze
With moveless hands
And face and gaze,
Then turns to go . . .
And what does he see when he gazes so?

II

They say he sees as an instant thing
More clear than to-day,
A sweet soft scene
That was once in play
By that briny green;
Yes, notes alway
Warm, real, and keen,
What his back years bring—
A phantom of his own figuring.

III

Of this vision of his they might say more:
Not only there
Does he see this sight,
But everywhere
In his brain—day, night,
As if on the air
It were drawn rose-bright—
Yea, far from that shore
Does he carry this vision of heretofore:

IV

A ghost-girl-rider. And though, toil-tried,
He withers daily,
Time touches her not,
But she still rides gaily
In his rapt thought
On that shagged and shaly
Atlantic spot,
And as when first eyed
Draws rein and sings to the swing of the tide.

1913

The Prospect

The twigs of the birch imprint the December sky
Like branching veins upon a thin old hand;
I think of summer-time, yes, of last July,
When she was beneath them, greeting a gathered band
Of the urban and bland.

Iced airs wheeze through the skeletoned hedge from the north,
With steady snores, and a numbing that threatens snow,
And skaters pass; and merry boys go forth
To look for slides. But well, well do I know
Whither I would go!

December 1912

Proud Songsters

The thrushes sing as the sun is going,
And the finches whistle in ones and pairs,
And as it gets dark loud nightingales
        In bushes
Pipe, as they can when April wears,
    As if all Time were theirs.

These are brand-new birds of twelve-months' growing,
Which a year ago, or less than twain,
No finches were, nor nightingales,
        Nor thrushes,
But only particles of grain,
    And earth, and air, and rain.

Rain on a Grave

Clouds spout upon her
  Their waters amain
  In ruthless disdain,—
Her who but lately
  Had shivered with pain
As at touch of dishonour
If there had lit on her
So coldly, so straightly
  Such arrows of rain:

One who to shelter
  Her delicate head
Would quicken and quicken
  Each tentative tread
If drops chanced to pelt her
  That summertime spills
  In dust-paven rills
When thunder-clouds thicken
  And birds close their bills.

Would that I lay there
  And she were housed here!
Or better, together
Were folded away there
Exposed to one weather
We both,—who would stray there
When sunny the day there,
  Or evening was clear
  At the prime of the year.

Soon will be growing
  Green blades from her mound,
And daisies be showing
  Like stars on the ground,
Till she form part of them—
Ay—the sweet heart of them,
Loved beyond measure
With a child's pleasure
  All her life's round.

31 Jan. 1913

Regret Not Me

Regret not me;
  Beneath the sunny tree
I lie uncaring, slumbering peacefully.

Swift as the light
  I flew my faery flight;
Ecstatically I moved, and feared no night.

I did not know
  That heydays fade and go,
But deemed that what was would be always so.

I skipped at morn
Between the yellowing corn,
Thinking it good and glorious to be born.

I ran at eves
Among the piled-up sheaves,
Dreaming. 'I grieve not, therefore nothing grieves.'

Now soon will come
The apple, pear, and plum,
And hinds will sing, and autumn insects hum.

Again you will fare
To cider-makings rare,
And junketings; but I shall not be there.

Yet gaily sing
Until the pewter ring
Those songs we sang when we went gipsying.

And lightly dance
Some triple-timed romance
In coupled figures, and forget mischance;

And mourn not me
Beneath the yellowing tree;
For I shall mind not, slumbering peacefully.

Reminiscences of a Dancing Man

I

Who now remembers Almack's balls—
    Willis's sometime named—
In those two smooth-floored upper halls
    For faded ones so famed?
Where as we trod to trilling sound
The fancied phantoms stood around,
    Or joined us in the maze,
Of the powdered Dears from Georgian years,
Whose dust lay in sightless sealed-up biers,
    The fairest of former days.

II

Who now remembers gay Cremorne,
    And all its jaunty jills,
And those wild whirling figures born
    Of Jullien's grand quadrilles?
With hats on head and morning coats
There footed to his prancing notes
    Our partner-girls and we;
And the gas-jets winked, and the lustres clinked,
And the platform throbbed as with arms enlinked
    We moved to the minstrelsy.

III

Who now recalls those crowded rooms
    Of old yclept 'The Argyle',
Where to the deep Drum-polka's booms
    We hopped in standard style?
Whither have danced those damsels now!
Is Death the partner who doth moue
    Their wormy chaps and bare?
Do their spectres spin like sparks within
The smoky halls of the Prince of Sin
    To a thunderous Jullien air?

The Ruined Maid

'O 'melia, my dear, this does everything crown!
Who could have supposed I should meet you in Town?
And whence such fair garments, such prosperi-ty?'—
'O didn't you know I'd been ruined?' said she.

—'You left us in tatters, without shoes or socks,
Tired of digging potatoes, and spudding up docks;
And now you've gay bracelets and bright feathers three!'—
'Yes: that's how we dress when we're ruined,' said she.

—'At home in the barton you said "thee" and "thou",
And "thik oon", and "theäs oon", and "t'other"; but now
Your talking quite fits 'ee for high compa-ny!'—
'Some polish is gained with one's ruin,' said she.

—'Your hands were like paws then, your face blue and bleak
But now I'm bewitched by your delicate cheek,
And your little gloves fit as on any la-dy!'—
'We never do work when we're ruined,' said she.

—'You used to call home-life a hag-ridden dream,
And you'd sigh, and you'd sock; but at present you seem
To know not of megrims or melancho-ly!'—
'True. One's pretty lively when ruined,' said she.

—'I wish I had feathers, a fine sweeping gown,
And a delicate face, and could strut about Town!'—
'My dear—a raw country girl, such as you be,
Cannot quite expect that. You ain't ruined,' said she.

Westbourne Park Villas, 1866

The Second Visit

Clack, clack, clack, went the mill-wheel as I came,
And she was on the bridge with the thin hand-rail,
And the miller at the door, and the ducks at mill-tail;
I come again years after, and all there seems the same.

And so indeed it is: the apple-tree'd old house,
And the deep mill-pond, and the wet wheel clacking,
And a woman on the bridge, and white ducks quacking,
And the miller at the door, powdered pale from boots to brows.

But it's not the same miller whom long ago I knew,
Nor are they the same apples, nor the same drops that dash
Over the wet wheel, nor the ducks below that splash,
Nor the woman who to fond plaints replied, 'You know I do!'

Self-Unconscious

Along the way
He walked that day,
Watching shapes that reveries limn,
And seldom he
Had eyes to see
The moment that encompassed him.

Bright yellowhammers
Made mirthful clamours,
And billed long straws with a bustling air,
And bearing their load
Flew up the road
That he followed, alone, without interest there.

From bank to ground
And over and round
They sidled along the adjoining hedge;
Sometimes to the gutter
Their yellow flutter
Would dip from the nearest slatestone ledge.

The smooth sea-line
With a metal shine,
And flashes of white, and a sail thereon,
He would also descry
With a half-wrapt eye
Between the projects he mused upon.

Yes, round him were these
Earth's artistries,
But specious plans that came to his call
Did most engage
His pilgrimage,
While himself he did not see at all.

Dead now as sherds
Are the yellow birds,
And all that mattered has passed away;
Yet God, the Elf,
Now shows him that self
As he was, and should have been shown, that day.

O it would have been good
Could he then have stood
At a clear-eyed distance, and conned the whole,
But now such vision
Is mere derision,
Nor soothes his body nor saves his soul.

Not much, some may
Incline to say,
To see therein, had it all been seen.
Nay! he is aware
A thing was there
That loomed with an immortal mien.

Near Bossiney

The Self-Unseeing

Here is the ancient floor,
Footworn and hollowed and thin,
Here was the former door
Where the dead feet walked in.

She sat here in her chair,
Smiling into the fire;
He who played stood there,
Bowing it higher and higher.

Childlike, I danced in a dream;
Blessings emblazoned that day;
Everything glowed with a gleam;
Yet we were looking away!

A Sheep Fair

The day arrives of the autumn fair,
And torrents fall,
Though sheep in throngs are gathered there,
Ten thousand all,
Sodden, with hurdles round them reared:
And, lot by lot, the pens are cleared,
And the auctioneer wrings out his beard,
And wipes his book, bedrenched and smeared,
And rakes the rain from his face with the edge of his hand,
As torrents fall.

The wool of the ewes is like a sponge
With the daylong rain:
Jammed tight, to turn, or lie, or lunge,
They strive in vain.
Their horns are soft as finger-nails,
Their shepherds reek against the rails,
The tied dogs soak with tucked-in tails,
The buyers' hat-brims fill like pails,
Which spill small cascades when they shift their stand
In the daylong rain.

POSTSCRIPT

Time has trailed lengthily since met
At Pummery Fair
Those panting thousands in their wet
And woolly wear:
And every flock long since has bled,
And all the dripping buyers have sped,
And the hoarse auctioneer is dead,
Who 'Going—going!' so often said,
As he consigned to doom each meek, mewed band
At Pummery Fair.

The Shiver

Five lone clangs from the house-clock nigh,
And I woke with a sigh:
Stars wore west like a slow tide flowing,
And my lover had told yesternight of his going,—
That at this gray hour he'd be hasting by,

Starting betimes on a journey afar:—
So, casement ajar,
I eyed in the upland pasture his figure,
A dim dumb speck, growing darker and bigger,
Then smalling to nought where the nut-trees are.

He could not bend his track to my window, he'd said,
Being hurried ahead:
But I wished he had tried to!—and then felt a shiver,
Corpse-cold, as he sank toward the town by the river;
And back I went sadly and slowly to bed.

What meant my shiver while seeing him pass
As a dot on the grass
I surmised not then. But later I knew it
When came again he; and my words outdrew it,
As said he: 'It's hard for your bearing, alas!

'But I've seen, I have clasped, where the smart ships plough,
One of far brighter brow.
A sea-goddess. Shiver not. One far rarer
In gifts than I find thee; yea, warmer and fairer:—
I seek her again; and I love you not now.'

Snow in the Suburbs

Every branch big with it,
Bent every twig with it;
Every fork like a white web-foot;
Every street and pavement mute:
Some flakes have lost their way, and grope back upward, when
Meeting those meandering down they turn and descend again.
The palings are glued together like a wall,
And there is no waft of wind with the fleecy fall.

A sparrow enters the tree,
Whereon immediately
A snow-lump thrice his own slight size
Descends on him and showers his head and eyes,
And overturns him,
And near inurns him,
And lights on a nether twig, when its brush
Starts off a volley of other lodging lumps with a rush.

The steps are a blanched slope;
Up which, with feeble hope,
A black cat comes, wide-eyed and thin;
  And we take him in.

Something Tapped

Something tapped on the pane of my room
  When there was never a trace
Of wind or rain, and I saw in the gloom
  My weary Belovéd's face.

'O I am tired of waiting,' she said,
  'Night, morn, noon, afternoon;
So cold it is in my lonely bed,
  And I thought you would join me soon!'

I rose and neared the window-glass,
  But vanished thence had she:
Only a pallid moth, alas,
  Tapped at the pane for me.

August 1913

A Spot

In years defaced and lost,
Two sat here, transport-tossed,
Lit by a living love
The wilted world knew nothing of:
Scared momently
By gaingivings,
Then hoping things
That could not be. . . .

Of love and us no trace
Abides upon the place;
The sun and shadows wheel,
Season and season sereward steal;

Foul days and fair
Here, too, prevail,
And gust and gale
As everywhere.

But lonely shepherd souls
Who bask amid these knolls
May catch a faery sound
On sleepy noontides from the ground:
'O not again
Till Earth outwears
Shall love like theirs
Suffuse this glen!'

The Sunshade

Ah—it's the skeleton of a lady's sunshade,
Here at my feet in the hard rock's chink,
Merely a naked sheaf of wires! –
Twenty years have gone with their livers and diers
Since it was silked in its white or pink.

Noonshine riddles the ribs of the sunshade,
No more a screen from the weakest ray;
Nothing to tell us the hue of its dyes,
Nothing but rusty bones as it lies
In its coffin of stone, unseen till to-day.

Where is the woman who carried that sunshade
Up and down this seaside place?—
Little thumb standing against its stem,
Thoughts perhaps bent on a love-stratagem,
Softening yet more the already soft face!

Is the fair woman who carried that sunshade
A skeleton just as her property is,
Laid in the chink that none may scan?
And does she regret—if regret dust can—
The vain things thought when she flourished this?

Swanage Cliffs

Thoughts of Phena

At News of Her Death

Not a line of her writing have I,
Not a thread of her hair,
No mark of her late time as dame in her dwelling, whereby
I may picture her there;
And in vain do I urge my unsight
To conceive my lost prize
At her close, whom I knew when her dreams were upbrimming with light,
And with laughter her eyes.

What scenes spread around her last days,
Sad, shining, or dim?
Did her gifts and compassions enray and enarch her sweet ways
With an aureate nimb?
Or did life-light decline from her years,
And mischances control
Her full day-star; unease, or regret, or forebodings, or fears
Disennoble her soul?

Thus I do but the phantom retain
Of the maiden of yore
As my relic; yet haply the best of her—fined in my brain
It may be the more
That no line of her writing have I,
Nor a thread of her hair,
No mark of her late time as dame in her dwelling, whereby
I may picture her there.

March 1890

A Trampwoman's Tragedy

(182–)

I

From Wynyard's Gap the livelong day,
The livelong day,
We beat afoot the northward way
We had travelled times before.
The sun-blaze burning on our backs,
Our shoulders sticking to our packs,
By fosseway, fields, and turnpike tracks
We skirted sad Sedge-Moor.

II

Full twenty miles we jaunted on,
We jaunted on,—
My fancy-man, and jeering John,
And Mother Lee, and I.
And, as the sun drew down to west,
We climbed the toilsome Poldon crest,
And saw, of landskip sights the best,
The inn that beamed thereby.

III

For months we had padded side by side,
Ay, side by side
Through the Great Forest, Blackmoor wide,
And where the Parret ran.
We'd faced the gusts on Mendip ridge,
Had crossed the Yeo unhelped by bridge,
Been stung by every Marshwood midge,
I and my fancy-man.

IV

Lone inns we loved, my man and I,
        My man and I;
'King's Stag', 'Windwhistle' high and dry,
    'The Horse' on Hintock Green,
The cosy house at Wynyard's Gap,
'The Hut' renowned on Bredy Knap,
And many another wayside tap
    Where folk might sit unseen.

V

Now as we trudged—O deadly day,
        O deadly day!—
I teased my fancy-man in play
    And wanton idleness.
I walked alongside jeering John,
I laid his hand my waist upon;
I would not bend my glances on
    My lover's dark distress.

VI

Thus Poldon top at last we won,
        At last we won,
And gained the inn at sink of sun
    Far-famed as 'Marshal's Elm'.
Beneath us figured tor and lea,
From Mendip to the western sea—
I doubt if finer sight there be
    Within this royal realm.

VII

Inside the settle all a-row—
        All four a-row
We sat, I next to John, to show
    That he had wooed and won.
And then he took me on his knee,
And swore it was his turn to be
My favourite mate, and Mother Lee
    Passed to my former one.

VIII

Then in a voice I had never heard,
I had never heard,
My only Love to me: 'One word,
My lady, if you please!
Whose is the child you are like to bear?—
His? After all my months o' care?'
God knows 'twas not! But, O despair!
I nodded—still to tease.

IX

Then up he sprung, and with his knife—
And with his knife
He let out jeering Johnny's life,
Yes; there, at set of sun.
The slant ray through the window nigh
Gilded John's blood and glazing eye,
Ere scarcely Mother Lee and I
Knew that the deed was done.

X

The taverns tell the gloomy tale,
The gloomy tale,
How that at Ivel-chester jail
My Love, my sweetheart swung;
Though stained till now by no misdeed
Save one horse ta'en in time o' need;
(Blue Jimmy stole right many a steed
Ere his last fling he flung.)

XI

Thereaft I walked the world alone,
Alone, alone!
On his death day I gave my groan
And dropped his dead-born child.
'Twas nigh the jail, beneath a tree,
None tending me; for Mother Lee
Had died at Glaston, leaving me
Unfriended on the wild.

XII

And in the night as I lay weak,
    As I lay weak,
The leaves a-falling on my cheek,
    The red moon low declined—
The ghost of him I'd die to kiss
Rose up and said: 'Ah, tell me this!
Was the child mine, or was it his?
    Speak, that I rest may find!'

XIII

O doubt not but I told him then,
    I told him then,
That I had kept me from all men
    Since we joined lips and swore.
Whereat he smiled, and thinned away
As the wind stirred to call up day . . .
—'Tis past! And here alone I stray
    Haunting the Western Moor.

NOTES.—'Windwhistle' (Stanza IV). The highness and dryness of Windwhistle Inn was impressed upon the writer two or three years ago, when, after climbing on a hot afternoon to the beautiful spot near which it stands and entering the inn for tea, he was informed by the landlady that none could be had, unless he would fetch water from a valley half a mile off, the house containing not a drop owing to its situation. However, a tantalizing row of full barrels behind her back testified to a wetness of a certain sort, which was not at that time desired.

'Marshal's Elm' (Stanza VI), so picturesquely situated, is no longer an inn, though the house, or part of it, still remains. It used to exhibit a fine old swinging sign.

'Blue Jimmy' (Stanza X) was a notorious horse-stealer of Wessex in those days, who appropriated more than a hundred horses before he was caught, among others one belonging to a neighbour of the writer's grandfather. He was hanged at the now demolished Ivel-chester or Ilchester jail above mentioned—that building formerly of so many sinister associations in the minds of the local peasantry, and the continual haunt of fever, which at last led to its condemnation. Its site is now an innocent-looking green meadow.

April 1902

Transformations

Portion of this yew
Is a man my grandsire knew,
Bosomed here at its foot:
This branch may be his wife,
A ruddy human life
Now turned to a green shoot.

These grasses must be made
Of her who often prayed,
Last century, for repose;
And the fair girl long ago
Whom I often tried to know
May be entering this rose.

So, they are not underground,
But as nerves and veins abound
In the growths of upper air,
And they feel the sun and rain,
And the energy again
That made them what they were!

Under the Waterfall

'Whenever I plunge my arm, like this,
In a basin of water, I never miss
The sweet sharp sense of a fugitive day
Fetched back from its thickening shroud of gray.
Hence the only prime
And real love-rhyme
That I know by heart,
And that leaves no smart,

Is the purl of a little valley fall
About three spans wide and two spans tall
Over a table of solid rock,
And into a scoop of the self-same block;
The purl of a runlet that never ceases
In stir of kingdoms, in wars, in peaces;
With a hollow boiling voice it speaks
And has spoken since hills were turfless peaks.'

'And why gives this the only prime
Idea to you of a real love-rhyme?
And why does plunging your arm in a bowl
Full of spring water, bring throbs to your soul?'

'Well, under the fall, in a crease of the stone,
Though where precisely none ever has known,
Jammed darkly, nothing to show how prized,
And by now with its smoothness opalized,
Is a drinking-glass:
For, down that pass
My lover and I
Walked under a sky
Of blue with a leaf-wove awning of green,
In the burn of August, to paint the scene,
And we placed our basket of fruit and wine
By the runlet's rim, where we sat to dine;
And when we had drunk from the glass together,
Arched by the oak-copse from the weather,
I held the vessel to rinse in the fall,
Where it slipped, and sank, and was past recall,
Though we stooped and plumbed the little abyss
With long bared arms. There the glass still is.
And, as said, if I thrust my arm below
Cold water in basin or bowl, a throe
From the past awakens a sense of that time,
And the glass we used, and the cascade's rhyme.

The basin seems the pool, and its edge
The hard smooth face of the brook-side ledge,
And the leafy pattern of china-ware
The hanging plants that were bathing there.

'By night, by day, when it shines or lours,
There lies intact that chalice of ours,
And its presence adds to the rhyme of love
Persistently sung by the fall above.
No lip has touched it since his and mine
In turns therefrom sipped lovers' wine.'

The Voice

Woman much missed, how you call to me, call to me,
Saying that now you are not as you were
When you had changed from the one who was all to me,
But as at first, when our day was fair.

Can it be you that I hear? Let me view you, then,
Standing as when I drew near to the town
Where you would wait for me: yes, as I knew you then,
Even to the original air-blue gown!

Or is it only the breeze, in its listlessness
Travelling across the wet mead to me here,
You being ever dissolved to wan wistlessness,
Heard no more again far or near?

Thus I; faltering forward,
Leaves around me falling,
Wind oozing thin through the thorn from norward,
And the woman calling.

December 1912

Voices from Things Growing in a Churchyard

These flowers are I, poor Fanny Hurd,
Sir or Madam,
A little girl here sepultured.
Once I flit-fluttered like a bird
Above the grass, as now I wave
In daisy shapes above my grave,
All day cheerily,
All night eerily!

– I am one Bachelor Bowring, 'Gent',
Sir or Madam;
In shingled oak my bones were pent;
Hence more than a hundred years I spent
In my feat of change from a coffin-thrall
To a dancer in green as leaves on a wall,
All day cheerily,
All night eerily!

—I, these berries of juice and gloss,
Sir or Madam,
Am clean forgotten as Thomas Voss;
Thin-urned, I have burrowed away from the moss
That covers my sod, and have entered this yew,
And turned to clusters ruddy of view,
All day cheerily,
All night eerily!

—The Lady Gertrude, proud, high-bred,
Sir or Madam,
Am I—this laurel that shades your head;
Into its veins I have stilly sped,
And made them of me; and my leaves now shine,
As did my satins superfine,
All day cheerily,
All night eerily!

—I who as innocent withwind climb,
Sir or Madam,
Am one Eve Greensleeves, in olden time
Kissed by men from many a clime,
Beneath sun, stars, in blaze, in breeze,
As now by glowworms and by bees,
All day cheerily,
All night eerily![1]

—I'm old Squire Audeley Grey, who grew,
Sir or Madam,
Aweary of life, and in scorn withdrew;
Till anon I clambered up anew
As ivy-green, when my ache was stayed,
And in that attire I have longtime gayed
All day cheerily,
All night eerily!

—And so these maskers breathe to each
Sir or Madam
Who lingers there, and their lively speech
Affords an interpreter much to teach,
As there murmurous accents seem to come
Thence hitheraround in a radiant hum,
All day cheerily,
All night eerily!

[1] It was said her real name was Eve Trevillian or Trevelyan; and that she was the handsome mother of two or three illegitimate children, *circa* 1784–95.

We Are Getting to the End

We are getting to the end of visioning
The impossible within this universe,
Such as that better whiles may follow worse,
And that our race may mend by reasoning.

We know that even as larks in cages sing
Unthoughtful of deliverance from the curse
That holds them lifelong in a latticed hearse,
We ply spasmodically our pleasuring.

And that when nations set them to lay waste
Their neighbours' heritage by foot and horse,
And hack their pleasant plains in festering seams,
They may again,—not warely, or from taste,
But tickled mad by some demonic force.—
Yes. We are getting to the end of dreams!

Weathers

I

This is the weather the cuckoo likes,
  And so do I;
When showers betumble the chestnut spikes,
  And nestlings fly:
And the little brown nightingale bills his best,
And they sit outside at 'The Travellers' Rest',
And maids come forth sprig-muslin drest,
And citizens dream of the south and west,
  And so do I.

II

This is the weather the shepherd shuns,
  And so do I;
When beeches drip in browns and duns,
  And thresh, and ply;
And hill-hid tides throb, throe on throe,
And meadow rivulets overflow,
And drops on gate-bars hang in a row,
And rooks in families homeward go,
  And so do I.

We Field-Women

How it rained
When we worked at Flintcomb-Ash,
And could not stand upon the hill
Trimming swedes for the slicing-mill.
The wet washed through us—plash, plash, plash:
How it rained!

How it snowed
When we crossed from Flintcomb-Ash
To the Great Barn for drawing reed,
Since we could nowise chop a swede.—
Flakes in each doorway and casement-sash:
How it snowed!

How it shone
When we went from Flintcomb-Ash
To start at dairywork once more
In the laughing meads, with cows three-score,
And pails, and songs, and love—too rash:
How it shone!

We Sat at the Window

We sat at the window looking out,
And the rain came down like silken strings
That Swithin's day. Each gutter and spout
Babbled unchecked in the busy way
Of witless things:
Nothing to read, nothing to see
Seemed in that room for her and me
On Swithin's day.

We were irked by the scene, by our own selves; yes,
For I did not know, nor did she infer
How much there was to read and guess
By her in me, and to see and crown
    By me in her.
Wasted were two souls in their prime,
And great was the waste, that July time
    When the rain came down.

Wessex Heights

(1896)

There are some heights in Wessex, shaped as if by a kindly hand
For thinking, dreaming, dying on, and at crises when I stand,
Say, on Ingpen Beacon eastward, or on Wylls-Neck westwardly,
I seem where I was before my birth, and after death may be.

In the lowlands I have no comrade, not even the lone man's friend—
Her who suffereth long and is kind; accepts what he is too weak to mend:
Down there they are dubious and askance; there nobody thinks as I,
But mind-chains do not clank where one's next neighbour is the sky.

In the towns I am tracked by phantoms having weird detective ways—
Shadows of beings who fellowed with myself of earlier days:
They hang about at places, and they say harsh heavy things—
Men with a wintry sneer, and women with tart disparagings.

Down there I seem to be false to myself, my simple self that was,
And is not now, and I see him watching, wondering what crass
 cause
Can have merged him into such a strange continuator as this,
Who yet has something in common with himself, my chrysalis.

I cannot go to the great grey Plain; there's a figure against the
 moon,
Nobody sees it but I, and it makes my breast beat out of tune;
I cannot go to the tall-spired town, being barred by the forms
 now passed
For everybody but me, in whose long vision they stand there
 fast.

There's a ghost at Yell'ham Bottom chiding loud at the fall of
 the night,
There's a ghost in Froom-side Vale, thin-lipped and vague, in a
 shroud of white,
There is one in the railway train whenever I do not want it near,
I see its profile against the pane, saying what I would not hear.

As for one rare fair woman, I am now but a thought of hers,
I enter her mind and another thought succeeds me that she
 prefers;
Yet my love for her in its fulness she herself even did not know;
Well, time cures hearts of tenderness, and now I can let her go.

So I am found on Ingpen Beacon, or on Wylls-Neck to the
 west,
Or else on homely Bulbarrow, or little Pilsdon Crest,
Where men have never cared to haunt, nor women have
 walked with me,
And ghosts then keep their distance; and I know some liberty.

When I Set Out for Lyonnesse

(1870)

When I set out for Lyonnesse,
  A hundred miles away,
  The rime was on the spray,
And starlight lit my lonesomeness
When I set out for Lyonnesse
  A hundred miles away.

What would bechance at Lyonnesse
  While I should sojourn there
  No prophet durst declare,
Nor did the wisest wizard guess
What would bechance at Lyonnesse
  While I should sojourn there.

When I came back from Lyonnesse
  With magic in my eyes,
  All marked with mute surmise
My radiance rare and fathomless,
When I came back from Lyonnesse
  With magic in my eyes!

When Oats Were Reaped

That day when oats were reaped, and wheat was ripe, and
    barley ripening,
  The road-dust hot, and the bleaching grasses dry,
   I walked along and said,
While looking just ahead to where some silent people lie:

‘I wounded one who’s there, and now know well I wounded her;
But, ah, she does not know that she wounded me!’
And not an air stirred,
Nor a bill of any bird; and no response accorded she.

August 1913

Where the Picnic Was

Where we made the fire
In the summer time
Of branch and briar
On the hill to the sea,
I slowly climb
Through winter mire,
And scan and trace
The forsaken place
Quite readily.

Now a cold wind blows,
And the grass is gray,
But the spot still shows
As a burnt circle—aye,
And stick-ends, charred,
Still strew the sward
Whereon I stand,
Last relic of the band
Who came that day!

Yes I am here
Just as last year,
And the sea breathes brine
From its strange straight line
Up hither, the same
As when we four came.

—But two have wandered far
From this grassy rise
Into urban roar
Where no picnics are,
And one—has shut her eyes
For evermore.

The Whitewashed Wall

Why does she turn in that shy soft way
 Whenever she stirs the fire,
And kiss to the chimney-corner wall,
 As if entranced to admire
Its whitewashed bareness more than the sight
 Of a rose in richest green?
I have known her long, but this raptured rite
 I never before have seen.

—Well, once when her son cast his shadow there,
 A friend took a pencil and drew him
Upon that flame-lit wall. And the lines
 Had a lifelike semblance to him.
And there long stayed his familiar look;
 But one day, ere she knew,
The whitener came to cleanse the nook,
 And covered the face from view.

'Yes,' he said: 'My brush goes on with a rush,
 And the draught is buried under;
When you have to whiten old cots and brighten,
 What else can you do, I wonder?'
But she knows he's there. And when she yearns
 For him, deep in the labouring night,
She sees him as close at hand, and turns
 To him under his sheet of white.

Who's in the Next Room?

'Who's in the next room?—who?
I seemed to see
Somebody in the dawning passing through,
Unknown to me.'
'Nay: you saw nought. He passed invisibly.'

'Who's in the next room?—who?
I seem to hear
Somebody muttering firm in a language new
That chills the ear.'
'No: you catch not his tongue who has entered there.'

'Who's in the next room?—who?
I seem to feel
His breath like a clammy draught, as if it drew
From the Polar Wheel.'
'No: none who breathes at all does the door conceal.'

'Who's in the next room?—who?
A figure wan
With a message to one in there of something due?
Shall I know him anon?'
'Yea he; and he brought such; and you'll know him anon.

The Wind's Prophecy

I travel on by barren farms,
And gulls glint out like silver flecks
Against a cloud that speaks of wrecks,
And bellies down with black alarms.
I say: 'Thus from my lady's arms
I go; those arms I love the best!'
The wind replies from dip and rise,
'Nay; toward her arms thou journeyest.'

A distant verge morosely gray
Appears, while clots of flying foam
Break from its muddy monochrome,
And a light blinks up far away.
I sigh: 'My eyes now as all day
Behold her ebon loops of hair!'
Like bursting bonds the wind responds,
'Nay, wait for tresses flashing fair!'

From tides the lofty coastlands screen
Come smitings like the slam of doors,
Or hammerings on hollow floors,
As the swell cleaves through caves unseen.
Say I: 'Though broad this wild terrene,
Her city home is matched of none!'
From the hoarse skies the wind replies:
'Thou shouldst have said her sea-bord one.'

The all-prevailing clouds exclude
The one quick timorous transient star;
The waves outside where breakers are
Huzza like a mad multitude.
'Where the sun ups it, mist-imbued,'
I cry, 'there reigns the star for me!'
The wind outshrieks from points and peaks:
'Here, westward, where it downs, mean ye!'

Yonder the headland, vulturine,
Snores like old Skrymer in his sleep,
And every chasm and every steep
Blackens as wakes each pharos-shine.
'I roam, but one is safely mine,'
I say. 'God grant she stay my own!'
Low laughs the wind as if it grinned:
'Thy Love is one thou'st not yet known.'

Rewritten from an old copy

The Year's Awakening

How do you know that the pilgrim track
Along the belting zòdiac
Swept by the sun in his seeming rounds
Is traced by now to the Fishés' bounds
And into the Ram, when weeks of cloud
Have wrapt the sky in a clammy shroud,
And never as yet a tinct of spring
Has shown in the earth's apparelling;
O vespering bird, how do you know,
How do you know?

How do you know, deep underground,
Hid in your bed from sight and sound,
Without a turn in temperature,
With weather life can scarce endure,
That light has won a fraction's strength,
And day put on some moments' length,
Whereof in merest rote will come,
Weeks hence, mild airs that do not numb;
O crocus root, how do you know,
How do you know?

February 1910

The Young Glass-Stainer

'These Gothic windows, how they wear me out
With cusp and foil, and nothing straight or square,
Crude colours, leaden borders roundabout,
And fitting in Peter here, and Matthew there!

'What a vocation! Here do I draw now
The abnormal, loving the Hellenic norm;
Martha I paint, and dream of Hera's brow,
Mary, and I think of Aphrodite's form.'

Nov. 1893

Zermatt
To the Matterhorn

(June–July 1897)

Thirty-two years since, up against the sun,
Seven shapes, thin atomies to lower sight,
Labouringly leapt and gained thy gabled height,
And four lives paid for what the seven had won.

They were the first by whom the deed was done,
And when I look at thee, my mind takes flight
To that day's tragic feat of manly might,
As though, till then, of history thou hadst none.

Yet ages ere men topped thee, late and soon
Thou didst behold the planets lift and lower;
Saw'st, maybe, Joshua's pausing sun and moon,
And the betokening sky when Caesar's power
Approached its bloody end; yea, even that Noon
When darkness filled the earth till the ninth hour.

NOTES

p. 1 After a Journey
Written in 1913 after a visit to the north Cornish coast, where Hardy had met his first wife (she died November 1912).

p. 2 Afternoon Service at Mellstock
Mellstock: Stinsford. The poem describes Hardy in the parish church with his family.
Tate-and-Brady: a metrical version of the Psalms.

p. 2 Afterwards
The dewfall hawk: the nightjar or nighthawk. Much of the early imagery is taken from Hardy's novel *The Return of the Native.*

p. 3 An August Midnight
dumbledore: cockchafer beetle.

p. 4 At Castle Boterel
Castle Boterel: Boscastle, north Cornwall.

p. 5 At the Word "Farewell"
According to Hardy, this poem is 'literally true'.

p. 6 Autumn in King's Hintock Park
King's Hintock is Melbury Osmond, Dorset, where Hardy's mother was born.

p. 7 Beeny Cliff
On the north Cornish coast.

p. 9 Beyond the Last Lamp
Thirty years: written in 1911, the poem describes an incident in 1881, when Hardy lived in the London suburb of Tooting.

p. 12 A Broken Appointment
Probably associated with Mrs. Henniker, with whom Hardy was in love in his fifties.

p. 15 A Confession to a Friend in Trouble
Probably refers to Hardy's early friend H. M. Moule, who had troubles with drink and women, and who eventually committed suicide.

p. 16 The Conformers
cohue: a body of people.

p. 17 The Convergence of the Twain
On 15 April 1912, the liner *Titanic* sank while on her maiden voyage after a collision with an iceberg, with the loss of two-thirds of those aboard. Hardy wrote the poem to be printed in aid of the 'Titanic Disaster Fund'.

p. 22 The Dead Man Walking
*my friend:*H. M. Moule (see above).
my Love's heart hardened/In hate of me: Hardy and his first wife suffered severe estrangement in the 1890s.

p. 23 A Death-Day Recalled
Beeny, Juliot, Vallency, Bos (Boscastle), Targan are cliffs, rivers, and places in north Cornwall associated with Hardy's first wife.

p. 24 The Dream Is—Which?
Another poem about Hardy's dead first wife.
heys: country dances with curving movements.

p. 25 Drummer Hodge
Suggested by the death in the South African War (1899–1902) of an actual drummer-boy from a village near Hardy's Dorset home.
kopje: hill or mound
veldt: plain
Karoo: a barren plateau
These are all South African terms.

p. 25 During Wind and Rain
The scenes and people of this poem are the various homes and the family of Hardy's first wife during her childhood in Plymouth. The idea was taken by Hardy from a book of manuscript 'Recollections' she left behind at her death.

p. 26 The Eve of Waterloo
A chorus from Hardy's epic *The Dynasts,* Part III, Act VI, sc. viii.
felloe-rim: rim of an artillery wheel.

Ind (India), Peninsular, Friedland, Austerlitz: campaigns and battles fought by Napoleon's troops.

p. 28 The Five Students

The 'students' of the poem never actually all met one another, except in Hardy's imagination. They probably are H. M. Moule (died 1873), Hardy's sweetheart Tryphena Sparks (1890), Moule's brother Henry (1904), and Hardy's first wife (1912). The survivor is, of course, Hardy.

p. 29 Friends Beyond

stillicide: dripping of water
grinterns: drainage ditches
city stage: coach from London
the Trine: the Trinity

p. 33 Green Slates

The scene is Penpethy slate-quarry in north Cornwall.

p. 35 Her Dilemma

poppy-head: ornamental carving at the top of an end of a seat in church.

p. 38 I Found Her Out There

Dundagel: Tintagel.

p. 42 The Impercipient

liefer: rather

p. 43 In a Waiting-Room

bagman: commercial traveller, rep.

p. 45 In the British Museum

Areopagus: Paul. According to Acts xvii, 19–23, St Paul preached to the Athenians at the Areopagus, a hill where the judicial court held its sittings.

p. 49 The Later Autumn

toadsmeat: a poisonous fungus

p. 50 Life and Death at Sunrise

call up the French Revolution: remember the outbreak of the French Revolution in 1789.

p. 51 Logs on the Hearth

Written in memory of Hardy's sister Mary, who died on 24 November 1915.

p. 53 Midnight on the Great Western
Hardy has a similar description in the novel *Jude the Obscure.*
p. 54 The Missed Train
onetime: once upon a time.
p. 55 Molly Gone
Another poem on the death of Hardy's sister, Mary.
Whitesheet . . . Lewsdon in the west: places in Dorset and Somerset, favourites of Hardy. See *Wessex Heights.*
p. 57 Near Lanivet, 1872
The incident which, according to Hardy, was 'literally true', occurred during the course of his engagement to his first wife in north Cornwall.
her crucified: probably by Hardy's attentions, after marriage, to other women.
p. 59 The Night of Trafalgar
Chorus from *The Dynasts.*
the Nothe: tall cliff overlooking Weymouth Bay.
p. 60 Nobody Comes
The date, 9 October 1924, gives significance to the poem. On that day, Florence, Hardy's second wife, was driven home by car from a London nursing-home where she had undergone an operation. Hardy's anxiety is reflected in the poem.
p. 62 Not Only I
Spoken by Hardy's dead first wife.
p. 63 Old Furniture
the nut: the bridge of a violin.
p. 64 The Oxen
Based on a superstition, told to Hardy by his mother, that on Christmas Eve the farm animals would kneel in memory of the birth of Jesus.
barton: farmyard.
p. 67 The Phantom Horsewoman
Another poem to Hardy's dead wife.
p. 72 Reminiscences of a Dancing Man
Almack's . . . Willis's: names of a dance-hall in King Street, near Covent Garden.

Cremorne: the Cremorne Gardens, Chelsea.
yclept: called.
The Argyll: a dancing place in Regent Street.
moue: In earliest Mss. 'mowe' or 'mow' meant make grimaces at.
chaps: cheeks.
Prince of Sin: the devil. Many of these dance-places were frequented by prostitutes.
Jullien: Louis Antoine Jullien (1812–60), a French composer of popular dance-music.

p. 73 The Ruined Maid
barton: see above, *The Oxen.*
hag-ridden: nightmare.

p. 76 A Sheep Fair
Pummery: Poundbury Hill, north-west of Dorchester.

p. 81 Thoughts of Phena
Written on the death of Hardy's cousin, Tryphena Sparks (1851–90).
nimb: nimbus or halo.
fined: refined, enobled.

p. 82 A Trampwoman's Tragedy
According to Hardy, the incidents of this narrative poem occured in 1827. The trampwoman's name was Mary Ann Taylor. Hardy believed this to be his most successful poem.

p. 86 Under the Waterfall
The poem is modelled closely on an incident described in the Ms. recollections of Hardy's first wife.

p. 90 We Are Getting to the End
whiles: times.
warely: consciously, deliberately.

p. 91 Weathers
hill-hid tides: the sea on the other side of the hill.

p. 92 We Field-Women
Based on scenes Hardy himself had described in his novel *Tess of the d'Urbervilles.*

p. 93 *Wessex Heights*

An enigmatic poem, known to be connected with Hardy's disillusion after the critics had attacked his novel *Jude The Obscure* (1895). One explanation might be that the 'heights' are those of poetry, which he now determined to write rather than any more prose, 'the lowlands'. The 'ghosts' of stanzas 6 and 7 are known to be four women, but only the last, in stanza 7, can be positively identified as Mrs. Henniker, (see above: *A Broken Appointment)*. The places mentioned are all in Dorset or in neighbouring counties.

p. 95 *When I Set Out For Lyonnesse*

Lyonnesse: Cornwall

p. 99 *The Wind's Prophecy*

This describes Hardy's journey to Cornwall in March 1870, when he met his first wife, the fair-haired Emma Gifford. The girl with "ebon loops of hair" is probably his dark-haired cousin, Tryphena Sparks (see above, *Thoughts of Phena*).

Skrymer: in Norse mythology a giant whose snores made a loud noise.

pharos: lighthouse.

p. 100 *The Year's Awakening*

Fishes . . . Ram: signs of the Zodiac, Pisces and Aries.

p. 101 *The Young Glass-Stainer*

cusp and foil: projecting point and small arc in a Gothic tracery window.

Peter . . . Matthew . . . Martha . . . Mary: New Testament figures.

Hera . . . Aphrodite: Greek goddesses.

p. 101 *Zermatt: To The Matterhorn*

The Matterhorn, a mountain (14,782 feet) on the border of Switzerland and Italy, was the scene of a famous tragedy in 1865, when four out of a party of seven climbers were killed. Hardy knew the leader of the climbers, E. M. Whymper, and on a visit to Zermatt at the foot of the mountain in 1897, he wrote this poem.

atomies: pigmies.

Joshua's pausing sun and moon: in the Old Testament story, the sun and moon stood still while the Jewish leader, Joshua, slaughtered his enemies.

The betokening sky: the sky was full of portents before the murder of Caesar, as described by Shakespeare in *Julius Caesar,* II, ii, 19–21.

darkness . . . the ninth hour: the darkness when Christ died, described il St. Mark's Gospel, XV, 33.

INDEX OF FIRST LINES

A load of brushes and baskets and cradles and chairs 61
A shaded lamp and a waving blind, 3
Ah—it's the skeleton of a lady's sunshade, 80
Along the way 74
'And now to God the Father,' he ends, 44
Around the house the flakes fly faster, 10
As I drive to the junction of lane and highway, 4

Beeny did not quiver, 23

Christmas Eve, and twelve of the clock. 64
Clack, clack, clack, went the mill-wheel as I came, 74
Clouds spout upon her 69

Every branch big with it, 78

Five lone clangs from the house-clock nigh, 77
From Wynyard's Gap the livelong day, 82

Gone are the lovers, under the bush 49

He does not think that I haunt here nightly: 34
He often would ask us 12
Here by the baring bough 6
Here is the ancient floor, 76
Here we broached the Christmas barrel, 37
Hereto I come to view a voiceless ghost; 1
Horses in horsecloths stand in a row 36
How do you know that the pilgrim track 100
How it rained 92
How I was caught 54
How she would have loved 47
How smartly the quarters of the hour march by 19

I am laughing by the brook with her, 24
I am the family face; 36
I am the one whom ringdoves see 37

I found her out there 38
I have lived with Shades so long, 40
I idly cut a parsley stalk, 64
I know not how it may be with others 63
I leant upon a copice gate 20
I look into my glass, 41
I marked when the weather changed, 60
I travel on by barren farms, 99
I went by footpath and by stile 66
In a solitude of the sea 17
In the third-class seat sat the journeying boy, 53
In the wild October night-time, when the wind raved round the land, 59
In years defaced and lost, 79
It happened once, before the duller 33

No more summer for Molly and me; 55
No; no; 65
Not a line of her writing have I, 81
Not only I 62

'O' melia, my dear, this does everything crown! 73
'O Passenger, pray list and catch 49
O the opal and the sapphire of that wandering western sea, 7
On afternoons of drowsy calm 2
On a morning sick as the day of doom 43
Only a man harrowing clods 47

'Peace upon earth!' was said. We sing it, 14
Portion of this yew 86

Queer are the ways of a man I know: 67

Regret not me; 70

She looked like a bird from a cloud 5
Something tapped on the pane of my room 79
Sweet cyder is a great thing, 32

That day when oats were reaped, and wheat was ripe, and barley ripening, 95
That with this bright believing band 42
The day arrives of the autumn fair, 76
The day is turning ghost, 14

The eyelids of eve fall together at last, 26
The fire advances along the log 51
The hills uncap their tops 50
The sparrow dips in his wheel-rut bath, 28
The two were silent in a sunless church, 35
The thrushes sing as the sun is going 69
The twigs of the birch imprint the December sky 68
There are some heights in Wessex, shaped as if by a kindly hand 93
There was a stunted handpost just on the crest, 57
These flowers are I, poor Fanny Hurd, 89
These Gothic windows, how they wear me out 101
They hail me as one living, 22
They sing their dearest songs— 25
They throw in Drummer Hodge, to rest 25
Thirty-two years since, up against the sun, 101
This is the weather the cuckoo likes 91
Tree leaves labour up and down 60

We are getting to the end of visioning 90
We sat at the window looking out, 92
We stood by a pond that winter day, 58
'What do you see in that time-touched stone, 45
What of the faith and fire within us 52
When I look forth at dawning, pool, 56
When I set out for Lyonnesse, 95
When the inmate stirs, the birds retire discreetly 11
When the Present has latched its postern behind my tremulous stay, 2
'Whenever I plunge my arm, like this, 86
Where we made the fire 96
While rain, with eve in partnership 9
Who now remembers Almack's balls— 72
'Who's in the next room?—who? 98
Why did you give no hint that night 31
Why does she turn in that shy soft way 97
William Dewy, Tranter Reuben, Farmer Ledlow late at plough, 29
Woman much missed, how you call to me, call to me, 88

Yes we'll wed, my little fay, 16
You did not come, 11
'You see those mothers squabbling there?' 46
Your troubles shrink not, though I feel them less 15